Empowering Life Skills for Teen Girls

Everything You Need to Thrive at Home, at School, and Out in the World - Confidence, Health, Money Management, and Essential Skills

Hannah Riley

Contents

CHAPTER ONE

Welcome Letters

A Personal Note to the Girl

Dear Supergirl,

Hey there! I'm so glad you're holding this book. It's been put together just for you to help you realize just how amazing you are. As you grow up, there are so many things to learn, feel, and experience, and I want you to know that every part of you is incredible and vital.

Growing up is like being on an adventure; sometimes, it can feel like you're unsure how to go. That's totally normal. Think of this book as your treasure map, guiding you to discover all the hidden treasures inside you. Each chapter is packed with tips, stories, and advice to help you become the best version of yourself.

So, let's explore right in and start this journey together.

1. You Are Unique and Powerful

There's no one else in the world quite like you. Your thoughts, feelings, and dreams are all your own. Embrace what makes you different. It's your super strength. You may have a quirky laugh, a creative mind, or a kind heart. Whatever it is, it's what makes YOU.

Take a moment to think about the things that make you unique. Write them down if you want. Celebrate them. These are the ingredients that make you a unique Supergirl.

2. Embrace Your Emotions

Growing up means feeling a lot of different emotions. Happiness, sadness, excitement, anger – they're all part of the package. It's okay to feel whatever you're feeling. What's important is to understand those feelings and find healthy ways to express them.

If you're happy, share that joy with others. If you're sad, talk to someone you trust. Sometimes, talking about what's on your mind can make a huge difference. Remember, it's okay to ask for help. Everyone needs a little support now and then.

3. Build Strong Relationships

Friends and family are like your support team. They cheer you on, help you when you're down, and celebrate your successes. Building solid relationships takes effort and kindness. Be a good listener, be honest, and show that you care.

Making new friends can be exciting but also a bit scary. Start with a smile and a simple hello. Be yourself, and you'll attract people who appreciate you for who you are. Remember, a good friend respects you and makes you feel good about yourself.

4. Take Care of Yourself

Your body and mind are like superheroes' tools. Taking care of them is crucial. Practice good hygiene—brush your teeth, wash your hands, and keep yourself clean. Eat nutritious foods that fuel your body and give you energy. Exercise regularly to keep your body strong and healthy.

But self-care isn't just about your body. It's about your mind, too. Take time to relax and do things that make you happy. Whether reading a book, drawing, playing sports, or just chilling out with music, find what works for you and make it a part of your routine.

5. Keep Learning and Growing

Every day is a new opportunity to learn something exciting. Stay curious. Ask questions. Explore new hobbies. School is a big part of learning, but it's not the only place you can grow. Life itself is full of lessons.

Don't be afraid of making mistakes. They're a natural part of learning. When things are unplanned, consider what you can learn from the experience. That's how you grow and become even stronger.

6. Stay Confident and Positive

Believing in yourself is one of the most effective ways to strengthen yourself. Confidence isn't about being perfect; it's about knowing you can handle whatever comes your way. Positive thinking can help you stay motivated and focused on your goals.

When you face challenges, remember that you have the strength to overcome them. Take a deep breath, remind yourself of your capabilities, and take things one step at a time. You've got this!

7. Dream Big and Plan for the Future

Your dreams are like stars guiding you through the night. Think about what you want to achieve, both in the short term and the long term. Write down your goals and plan to reach them. It could be something minor, like finishing a book, or something big, like a career aspiration.

Creating a vision board can be a fun way to visualize your dreams. Gather pictures, quotes, and anything else that inspires you. Place them on a board where you can see them every day. It's a constant reminder of what you're working towards.

8. Be Kind and Compassionate

Kindness is a super strength that can change the world. Treat others with respect and knowledge. Small acts of kindness, like a smile, a compliment, or helping someone in need, can make a big difference.

They said being compassionate means putting yourself in someone else's shoes. It's about knowing their feelings and showing empathy. Being kind and compassionate makes others feel good and enriches your life.

As you explore each chapter in this book, take your time to reflect on the information and how it applies to your life. Share your thoughts and experiences with those you trust. They can offer valuable insights and support as you grow.

Remember, you are capable of amazing things. The path ahead may have ups and downs. Still, you can overcome challenges and achieve your dreams with determination, resilience, and a positive attitude. So, get ready to release your inner superwoman and embrace the adventure of growing up!

A Special Message to the Parents

Dear Parents,

Hello and welcome. Thank you for taking an interest in this book, designed to support your daughter as she navigates the details of growing up. This guide aims to help her discover her inner strength, build essential life skills, and grow into a confident and strong young woman.

Your role in her journey is vital. Your support, guidance, and love form the foundation she builds. This book complements your efforts by providing practical advice, valuable tips, and strengthening messages customized for young girls.

Here's what we hope to achieve together:

1. Strengthen and Confidence

One of our primary goals is to help your daughter develop a strong sense of self-worth and confidence. We want her to recognize her unique qualities and understand that she has the strength to achieve her dreams. Your encouragement can reinforce these messages and help her build a positive self-image.

2. Emotional Intelligence

Understanding and managing emotions is a crucial part of growing up. This book provides tools and strategies to help your daughter navigate her feelings. We encourage you to create an open environment where she feels safe expressing her emotions and discussing her thoughts.

3. Communication Skills

Effective communication is essential for building strong relationships and achieving success. This book includes tips on expressing thoughts clearly and listening actively. You can support her by modeling good communication practices and encouraging open dialogue at home.

4. Building Healthy Relationships

Friendships and family relationships are critical to a happy and fulfilling life. This book emphasizes the importance of kindness, respect, and empathy in relationships. Encourage your daughter to value her connections and to be a good friend and family member.

5. Self-Care and Hygiene

Good hygiene and self-care are fundamental to health and well-being. This book offers practical advice on maintaining daily routines and caring for physical and mental health. Reinforce these habits at home by setting a good example and providing the necessary resources.

6. Growth Mindset

A growth mindset is about believing in the potential to learn and improve. This book promotes the idea that challenges are growth opportunities. Help your daughter adopt this mindset by celebrating her efforts, not just her achievements, and encouraging her to learn from setbacks.

7. Financial Literacy

Understanding money management is a valuable life skill. This book introduces concepts like budgeting, saving, and spending wisely. You can support her learning by discussing family finances age-appropriately and involving her in financial decisions where possible.

8. Household Responsibilities

Knowing how to manage household tasks is essential for independence. This book covers basic chores and home management skills. Encourage your daughter to take on responsibilities at home, creating a sense of contribution and capability.

9. Digital Literacy and Safety

Knowing how to use technology safely is crucial today. This book addresses safe internet practices and the responsible use of digital tools. Monitor her online activities, teach her about online safety, and set boundaries to protect her.

10. Creativity and Passion

Exploring creativity and pursuing passions can lead to a fulfilling life. This book encourages your daughter to find and nurture her interests. Support her by providing opportunities for creative expression and encouraging her to pursue activities she loves.

11. Goal Setting and Future Planning

Setting goals and planning for the future are essential steps toward achieving dreams. This book guides your daughter through identifying and working towards her goals. Discuss her aspirations with her and help her create a plan to achieve them.

12. Kindness and Compassion

Kindness and compassion are core values that contribute to a better world. This book highlights the importance of these traits. Lead by example, showing kindness in your actions and encouraging your daughter to be compassionate toward others.

As your daughter goes through this book, she will gain valuable insights and skills. Encourage her to share what she learns with you and to discuss how she can apply these lessons in her daily life. Your involvement and support are crucial to her success.

We hope this book is a helpful resource for you and your daughter. Together, you can navigate the challenges and celebrate the joys of growing up, helping her become the confident and muscular young woman she is meant to be.

Thank you for being a part of this journey and for supporting your daughter every step of the way.

CHAPTER TWO

Unleashing Your Inner Superwoman

Discovering Your Strengths

Hey there, Supergirl! Let's start this journey by discussing something significant: discovering your strengths. Everyone has special abilities, unique qualities, and hidden talents. These are the things that make you you. When you find your strengths, you can use them to shine brightly and make a difference in the world.

Understanding Strengths

Strengths are the things you are naturally good at or the qualities that come quickly to you. They can be anything from being a great listener to having a knack for solving puzzles. Sometimes, strengths are obvious, like being good at sports or music, but other times, they might be hidden and take some exploring.

Why Knowing Your Strengths is Important

Knowing your strengths can boost your confidence and help you feel good about yourself. It also helps you understand your capabilities and how you can contribute to your family, friends, and community. When you focus on your strengths, you're more likely to be happy and successful in what you do.

How to Discover Your Strengths

1. **Self-Reflection**: Take some quiet time to think about what you enjoy and are good at. Ask yourself questions like:

   ○ What activities make me feel happy and energized?

   ○ What subjects do I excel in at school?

   ○ What tasks do I find easy that others might find challenging?

2. **Ask for Feedback**: Sometimes, others can see our strengths more clearly than we can. Ask your family, friends, and teachers about your strengths. You might be surprised by what they say!

3. **Try New Things**: Exploring new activities and hobbies can help you discover hidden talents. Don't hesitate to step out

of your comfort zone and try something new. Whether it's a new sport, a musical instrument, or a craft, you might find a new strength you didn't know you had.

4. **Keep a Journal**: Write down your achievements and what you feel proud of. Over time, you'll start to see patterns and recognize your strengths. Journaling is a great way to track your progress and reflect on your growth.

Examples of Strengths

Strengths can come in many forms. Here are some examples to get you thinking:

- **Creative**: You might be great at drawing, writing stories, or developing new ideas.

- Analytical: You could have a knack for solving problems, knowing complex concepts, or thinking critically.

- **Social**: You may be good at making friends, listening to others, or leading a group.

- **Physical**: You might excel in sports, dancing, or other physical activities.

- Empathetic: You could be great at knowing how others feel and offering support.

Using Your Strengths

Once you've identified your strengths, the next step is to use them in your daily life. Here are some ways to put your strengths to work:

1. **Set Goals**: Use your strengths to set personal goals. For example, if you're good at writing, set a goal to write a short story or start a blog. If you're athletic, aim to join a sports team or improve your skills in a particular sport.

2. **Help Others**: Use your strengths to make a positive impact on those around you. If you're good at organizing, help plan a school event or organize a community cleanup. If you're empathetic, offer support to a friend who is going through a tough time.

3. **Pursue Hobbies**: Spend time doing activities that align with your strengths. This will bring you joy and help you improve your skills and grow even stronger.

4. **Challenge Yourself**: Use your strengths to take on new challenges. If you're a natural leader, volunteer to lead a group project at school. If you're analytical, tackle a complex math problem or science experiment.

Celebrating Your Strengths

Recognize and celebrate your achievements. Every time you use your strengths to overcome a challenge or reach a goal, take a moment to appreciate your hard work and success. Celebrate in a meaningful way, whether it's treating yourself to a favorite activity, sharing your achievement with loved ones, or simply reflecting on your progress.

Building a Strengths-Based Mindset

Developing a strengths-based mindset means focusing on what you're good at rather than dwelling on your weaknesses. Here's how you can cultivate this mindset:

1. **Positive Self-Talk**: Replace negative thoughts with positive affirmations. Instead of saying, "I can't do this," say, "I'm capable and will give it my best shot."

2. **Growth Mindset**: Believe your strengths can grow with effort and practice. Embrace challenges as opportunities to learn and improve.

3. **Celebrate Others**: Acknowledge and celebrate the strengths of those around you. This fosters a positive and supportive environment where everyone feels valued.

Real-Life Superwomen

To inspire you further, let's look at some real-life superwomen who discovered their strengths and used them to make a difference:

1. **Malala Yousafzai**: Malala is a Pakistani activist for girls' education. Even facing enormous challenges, she used her strength of courage and her strong voice to advocate for education and equal rights. She became the youngest-ever

Nobel Prize laureate.

2. **Greta Thunberg**: Greta is a young climate activist from Sweden. She discovered her strength in public speaking and her passion for the environment, leading to her global movement to address climate change. Her strength has inspired millions to act.

3. **Simone Biles**: Simone is an American gymnast with incredible athletic ability. She discovered her strength in gymnastics at a young age. She worked tirelessly to become one of the greatest gymnasts, winning numerous Olympic and World Championship medals.

These women started just like you, discovering their strengths and using them to create positive change. Their stories show that your strengths can lead you to greatness no matter where you come from or what obstacles you face.

Exercises to Discover Your Strengths

To help you on your journey, here are some exercises you can try:

1. **Strengths List**: Write down a list of things you enjoy doing and feel confident about. Ask yourself what activities make you lose track of time and bring you joy.

2. **Feedback Circle**: Ask three trusted people to tell you what they think your strengths are. Write down their responses and look for common themes.

3. **Strengths Journal**: Keep a journal where you write down your daily accomplishments and moments you felt proud of yourself. Reflect on these entries to identify your strengths.

Overcoming Self-Doubt

Everyone experiences self-doubt sometimes, but it's important not to let it hold you back. Here are some tips to overcome self-doubt:

1. **Challenge Negative Thoughts**: When negative thoughts creep in, challenge them with evidence of your past successes and strengths.

2. **Seek Support**: Talk to someone you trust about your doubts. They can offer encouragement and help you see your strengths more clearly.

3. **Practice Self-Compassion**: Be kind to yourself. Remember that everyone makes mistakes and faces challenges. Treat yourself with the same compassion you would offer a friend.

Discovering your strengths is a strength step towards becoming the superwoman you are meant to be. It's about recognizing what makes you unique and using those qualities to navigate the world with confidence and purpose. Take the time to explore, reflect, and celebrate your strengths. They are the keys to unlocking your full potential.

Now that you've discovered your strengths, let's move on to building self-esteem, which will help you feel even more confident and capable. You're doing great, Supergirl – keep shining!

Building Self-Esteem

Building self-esteem is like building a solid foundation for a house. It gives you the confidence and resilience to face life's challenges and pursue your dreams. High self-esteem means you believe in your worth and abilities, while low self-esteem can make you doubt yourself and hold you back.

Understanding Self-Esteem

Self-esteem is how you feel about yourself. Your thoughts, experiences, and interactions with others influence it. High self-esteem means you have a positive view of yourself and feel confident in your abilities. Low self-esteem can lead to feelings of inadequacy and self-doubt.

Why Self-Esteem Matters

Having high self-esteem is essential for many reasons:

1. Confidence: When you believe in yourself, you're more likely to take on new challenges and pursue your goals.

2. Resilience: High self-esteem helps you bounce back from setbacks and view failures as learning opportunities.

3. Healthy Relationships: People with high self-esteem are better at forming and maintaining positive relationships because they value themselves and others.

4. Happiness: A positive self-view contributes to overall happiness and well-being.

Building Self-Esteem

Building self-esteem takes time and effort, but it's a rewarding process. Here are some steps to help you build a strong sense of self-worth:

1. Practice Self-Compassion

Be kind to yourself, especially when things don't go as planned. Instead of criticizing yourself for mistakes, acknowledge that everyone makes them and focus on what you can learn. Treat yourself with the same kindness and knowing you would offer a friend.

2. Set Realistic Goals

Setting and achieving realistic goals can boost your confidence. Start with small, attainable goals and gradually move to bigger ones. Celebrate your accomplishments, no matter how small they may seem.

3. Focus on Your Strengths

As discussed in the previous section, recognizing and using your strengths can significantly boost your self-esteem. Spend time doing activities you excel at and enjoy. This reinforces your belief in your abilities.

4. Challenge Negative Thoughts

Everyone occasionally has negative thoughts, but it's important not to let them control you. When you think negatively, challenge those thoughts with positive affirmations and evidence of your strengths and past successes.

5. Surround Yourself with Positive Influences

The people you spend time with can significantly impact your self-esteem. Surround yourself with supportive, positive individuals who uplift and encourage you. Avoid people who bring you down or make you feel inadequate.

6. Take Care of Your Body

Physical health and self-esteem are closely linked. Eating nutritious foods, exercising regularly, and practicing good hygiene can make you feel better about yourself. When you care for your body, you also care for your mind.

7. Practice Gratitude

Gratitude can shift your focus from what you lack to what you have. Each day, take a moment to reflect on the things you're grateful for. This practice can help you develop a more positive outlook and fully appreciate your life and yourself.

8. Seek Support

If you're struggling with low self-esteem, don't hesitate to seek support from a trusted adult, such as a parent, teacher, or counselor. They can offer guidance and encouragement and help you see your worth.

Activities to Boost Self-Esteem

Here are some fun and practical activities to help you build self-esteem:

Affirmation Jar: Write positive affirmations about yourself on small pieces of paper and place them in a jar. Each day, pull out an affirmation and read it out loud to remind yourself of your strengths and worth.

1. Compliment Chain: Start a compliment chain with your friends or family. Each person compliments someone else, creating a circle of positivity and support.

2. Gratitude Journal: Keep a gratitude journal where you write down your gratitude for daily things. Include your accomplishments and positive qualities.

3. Vision Board: Create a vision board with images, quotes, and words that inspire you and represent your goals and dreams. Place it somewhere you can see it daily as a reminder of your potential.

4. Kindness Challenge: Set a goal to perform a certain number of acts of kindness each week. Helping others can boost your self-esteem and make you feel good about yourself.

Overcoming Obstacles to Self-Esteem

Everyone faces obstacles that can impact their self-esteem. Here's how to overcome some common challenges:

1. Peer Pressure: It's natural to want to fit in, but staying true to yourself is important. Remember that you are valuable just how you are and don't need to change to be accepted. Surround yourself with friends who appreciate you for who you are.

2. Comparison: It's easy to compare yourself to others, especially with the influence of social media. Remember that everyone's journey is different, and what you see online is often a highlight reel, not the whole story. Focus on your growth and accomplishments.

3. Perfectionism: Striving for perfection can lead to unnecessary stress and disappointment. Instead of aiming for perfection, aim for progress. Celebrate your efforts and improvements, and understand that mistakes are a natural part of learning.

4. Negative Self-Talk: Pay attention to your inner dialogue. If you notice negative self-talk, challenge it with positive affirmations and reminders of your strengths. Practice speaking to yourself with kindness and encouragement.

5. Failure: Failure is a part of life and an opportunity to learn and grow. When you experience failure, reflect on what you can learn from the situation and how to improve. Remember that one setback doesn't define you.

The Power of Positive Role Models

Positive role models can inspire and motivate you. Look for role models who demonstrate confidence, resilience, and kindness. They can be family members, teachers, friends, or public figures. Learn from their experiences and apply their lessons to your own life.

Building self-esteem is a continuous journey that involves recognizing your worth, embracing your strengths, and practicing self-compassion. It's about believing in yourself and your abilities and knowing that you are valuable just as you are. Following the steps and activities outlined in this chapter, you can develop a strong self-esteem that will strengthen you to face challenges, pursue your goals, and lead a fulfilling life.

Remember, Supergirl, you have the strength to build a strong foundation of self-esteem. Celebrate your uniqueness, focus on your strengths, and treat yourself kindly. You can be unique, and the world is waiting to see you shine.

This concludes the first section of your journey. You've learned to discover your strengths and build self-esteem, two crucial steps in releasing your inner superwoman. Keep these lessons to your heart as you grow and navigate the world confidently and gracefully. You're well on your way to becoming the incredible person you are meant to be. Keep shining, Supergirl!

CHAPTER THREE

Big Emotions

Understanding Feelings

Hello, Supergirl! Emotions can be like a rollercoaster ride. Sometimes, they lift us to the highest peaks of happiness and other times; they plunge us into the depths of sadness or frustration. Understanding and learning how to cope with your emotions is crucial to growing up. Let's explore the world's feelings and discover how to navigate them like a true superwoman.

What Are Emotions?

Emotions are your body's way of responding to different situations and experiences. They are complex reactions that involve your mind, body, and behavior. You might feel joy when you get a good grade, sadness when you lose a favorite toy, or anger when someone is mean to you. Emotions are a natural part of being human, and everyone experiences them.

Why Understanding Emotions is Important

Understanding your emotions can help you:

Communicate Better: When you know your feelings, you can express your needs and thoughts more clearly.

Make Better Decisions: Emotions can influence your choices. Recognizing them helps you make thoughtful decisions.

Build Stronger Relationships: Understanding your feelings and those of others can improve your relationships with friends, family, and teachers.

Improve Your Well-Being: Healthily managing your emotions can lead to a happier and more balanced life.

Identifying Emotions

Before you can manage your emotions, you need to identify them. Here are some common emotions and their characteristics:

Happiness: You might feel light and energetic and have a big smile. Happiness can come from spending time with friends, achieving a goal, or doing something you love.

Sadness can make you feel heavy, tired, or cry. It often comes from losing something important, disappointment, or loneliness.

Anger: Anger can make you tense and hot and make you want to yell or hit something. It usually arises when you feel threatened, frustrated, or mistreated.

Fear: Fear might make your heart race, your palms sweat, or your stomach feel tight. It often comes from facing something unknown or dangerous.

Surprise: Surprise can widen your eyes, open your mouth, and make your heart skip a beat. It happens when something unexpected occurs, whether it's good or bad.

Disgust: Disgust can make you wrinkle your nose, pull back, or feel sick to your stomach. It often happens when you encounter something unpleasant or offensive.

Emotional Vocabulary

A rich emotional vocabulary can help you identify and express your feelings more accurately. Here are some words to describe various emotions:

- **Joyful**: ecstatic, pleased, delighted, cheerful, content

- **Sad**: gloomy, heartbroken, melancholy, downcast, dejected

- **Angry**: furious, irritated, annoyed, resentful, enraged

- **Afraid**: terrified, anxious, nervous, scared, apprehensive

- **Surprised**: astonished, amazed, shocked, startled,

bewildered

- **Disgusted**: repulsed, appalled, offended, revolted, sickened

The Role of Emotions

Emotions serve essential functions in our lives. They can:

1. **Signal Needs**: Emotions can indicate that something needs attention. For example, hunger can make you irritable, signaling you need to eat.

2. **Guide Decisions**: Emotions can help you make decisions by highlighting what's important. Feeling anxious about a test might motivate you to study harder.

3. **Motivate Action**: Emotions can drive you to act. Anger over an injustice can inspire you to speak out or seek change.

4. **Improve Social Bonds**: Emotions help you connect with others. Sharing joy can strengthen friendships, while expressing sadness can bring comfort and support.

Managing Emotions

Managing your emotions doesn't mean ignoring or suppressing them. It means recognizing and knowing them and then responding healthily. Here are some strategies to help you manage your emotions effectively:

1. Recognize Your Emotions

The first step to managing your emotions is to recognize them. Pay attention to your body and mind. Notice how you're feeling and what might be causing those feelings. This awareness is the foundation for healthy emotional management.

2. Name Your Emotions

Once you recognize an emotion, name it. Saying, "I'm feeling angry," or "I'm feeling sad," can help you understand and process your feelings. It also makes communicating with others about what you're experiencing easier.

3. Accept Your Emotions

All emotions are valid, even the uncomfortable ones. Accept that it's okay to feel what you're feeling. Avoid judging yourself for your emotions. Remember, it's human to experience a wide range of feelings.

4. Understand the Cause

Try to understand what's causing your emotions. Are you angry because someone was unkind to you? Are you sad because you missed out on something important? Identifying the cause can help you address the root of your feelings.

5. Express Your Emotions

Find healthy ways to express your emotions. Talk to someone you trust, write in a journal, or engage in creative activities like drawing or playing music. Expressing your feelings can prevent them from building up and becoming overwhelming.

6. Practice Mindfulness

Mindfulness involves paying attention to the present moment without judgment. It can help you stay grounded and calm when emotions run high. Practice mindfulness by taking deep breaths, focusing on your senses, or meditating.

7. Use Positive Self-Talk

Replace negative thoughts with positive affirmations. Instead of saying, "I can't do this," say, "I'm capable and will give it my best shot." Positive self-talk can boost your confidence and help you manage emotions more effectively.

8. Take a Break

Sometimes, stepping away from a situation can help you calm down and gain perspective. Take a walk, listen to music, or do something you enjoy. A short break can give you the space to process your emotions.

9. Seek support

Don't hesitate to seek support from trusted adults, such as parents, teachers, or counselors. They can offer guidance, listen to your concerns, and help you navigate your emotions.

10. Practice Gratitude

Gratitude can shift your focus from negative emotions to positive ones. Each day, take a moment to reflect on the things you're grateful for. This practice can help you develop a positive outlook and improve your emotional well-being.

Healthy Ways to Cope

Coping with emotions healthily is essential for maintaining emotional balance and well-being. Let's explore effective coping strategies to help you manage your feelings and navigate life's challenges.

Physical Activity

Exercise is a solid way to cope with emotions. Physical activity releases endorphins, which are natural mood lifters. Whether going for a run, dancing, playing a sport, or even taking a brisk walk, moving your body can help you feel better.

Creative Expression

Engaging in creative activities can be a wonderful outlet for emotions. Drawing, painting, writing, playing music, or crafting can help you express your feelings healthily and productively. Let your creativity flow and see how it transforms your mood.

Breathing Exercises

Deep breathing exercises can help calm your mind and body. When you're feeling overwhelmed, try this simple breathing technique:

1. Sit or lie down in a comfortable position.

2. Close your eyes and take a deep breath through your nose, counting to four.

3. Hold your breath for a count of four.

4. Exhale slowly through your mouth, counting to four.

5. Repeat this process several times until you feel more relaxed.

Progressive Muscle Relaxation

Progressive muscle relaxation involves tensing and then relaxing different muscle groups. This technique can help reduce physical tension and promote relaxation. Here's how to do it:

1. Find a quiet, comfortable place to sit or lie down.

2. Start with your toes. Tense the muscles in your toes for a count of five, then release.

3. Move to your calves, thighs, stomach, chest, arms, and face, tensing and relaxing each muscle group.

4. Notice how your body feels more relaxed with each release.

Visualization

Visualization is a technique where you imagine a peaceful and calming scene. This can help you escape from stress and anxiety, even if just for a moment. Here's how to practice visualization:

1. Close your eyes and take a few deep breaths.

2. Picture a place where you feel safe and relaxed. It could be a beach, a forest, or a cozy room.

3. Think about this place's details – the sights, sounds, smells, and feelings.

4. Spend a few minutes immersed in this calming scene, then slowly open your eyes and return to the present moment.

Journaling

Writing about your feelings can help you process and understand them. Keep a journal where you can freely express your thoughts and emotions. You might write about your day, what's been on your mind, or how you feel about a particular situation. Journaling can provide clarity and help you find solutions to problems.

Talking to Someone

Sometimes, sharing your feelings with someone you trust can make a big difference. Talk to a friend, family member, or counselor about what you're going through. They can offer support, advice, and a different perspective.

Listening to Music

Music has a unique ability to influence our emotions. Create a playlist of your favorite songs that uplift your mood or help you relax. Listening to music can be a great way to cope with stress, sadness, or anger.

Spending Time in Nature

Being in nature can have a calming effect on your mind and body. Spend time outdoors, whether hiking, sitting in a park, or simply walking around your neighborhood. The fresh air and natural surroundings can help you feel more grounded and peaceful.

Practicing Self-Care

Self-care involves doing things that nurture your mind, body, and soul. Here are some self-care activities you can try:

- Take a warm bath with your favorite bubbles or bath salts.

- Read a book that you enjoy.

- Watch a funny movie or show.

- Do a puzzle or play a game.

- Spend time with a pet.

Setting Boundaries

Setting boundaries is an essential aspect of emotional health. It means knowing your limits and communicating them to others. For example, let your family and friends know if you need time to recharge. Setting boundaries can help you protect your emotional well-being and prevent burnout.

Practicing Mindfulness

Mindfulness involves paying attention to the present moment without judgment. It can help you stay calm and focused, even when emotions run high. Here are some mindfulness exercises you can try:

- **Mindful Breathing**: Focus on your breath as it goes in and out. Notice the sensation of the air entering and leaving your body.

- **Body Scan**: Close your eyes and slowly focus on different body parts, from your toes to your head. Notice any sensations, tension, or relaxation.

- **Mindful Eating**: Eat a snack slowly and mindfully. Pay attention to the taste, texture, and smell of the food. Notice how it feels as you chew and swallow.

Gratitude Practice

Practicing gratitude can shift your focus from negative emotions to positive ones. Each day, take a moment to reflect on the things you're grateful for. You can keep a gratitude journal or think about three things you're thankful for before bed.

Developing a Routine

Having a routine can provide structure and stability, which can be especially helpful during times of stress. Create a daily schedule that includes time for schoolwork, hobbies, exercise, and relaxation. A routine can help you feel more organized and in control.

Seeking Professional Help

If your emotions are overwhelming or challenging to manage, don't hesitate to seek professional help. A counselor, therapist, or psychologist can Support and teach you effective coping strategies. Remember, asking for help is a sign of strength, not weakness.

Putting It All Together

Now that we've explored various coping strategies let's combine them to create a plan that works for you. Here's a step-by-step guide to making your emotional management plan:

1. **Identify Your Triggers**: Consider the situations or experiences that trigger strong emotions. It could be school

stress, conflicts with friends, or changes at home.

2. **Choose Your Strategies**: Pick a few coping strategies from the list above that resonate with you. These should be techniques you feel comfortable trying that fit into your lifestyle.

3. **Create a Toolkit**: Put together a toolkit of resources that you can turn to when you're feeling overwhelmed. This could include a journal, a playlist of calming music, supportive people you can talk to, and any other items that help you feel better.

4. **Practice Regularly**: Coping strategies are most effective when practiced regularly. Make time for these activities in your daily routine, even when you're not feeling particularly stressed. This way, you'll be well-prepared to handle emotions when they arise.

5. **Reflect and Adjust**: Periodically evaluate how your coping strategies are working. If something needs to be helping, feel free to try a different approach. It's all about finding what works best for you.

Real-Life Supergirl's

To inspire you further, let's look at some real-life super girls who have learned to master their emotions and cope with challenges:

1. **Emma González**: Emma is a gun control advocate and survivor of the Parkland school shooting. She channeled her feelings into activism despite intense emotions and public scrutiny. Emma's strength and resilience have inspired many to act for change.

2. **Alex Scott**: Alex is a young cancer survivor who started Alex's Lemonade Stand to raise money for cancer research. Even while battling her illness, Alex found a way to turn her emotions into a positive force, raising millions of dollars and inspiring others to join her cause.

3. **Jazz Jennings**: Jazz is a transgender activist who has been open about her journey and emotions. Through her honesty and advocacy, Jazz has helped raise awareness and support for the LGBTQ+ community, showing incredible courage and resilience.

These young women faced significant challenges and intense emotions, yet they found ways to cope and make a positive impact. Their stories show that it's possible to master your emotions and use them as a source of strength.

Mastering big emotions is a vital skill that will help you navigate the ups and downs of life. By knowing your feelings and learning healthy coping methods, you can maintain emotional balance and well-being. Remember, feeling a wide range of emotions is okay, and finding strategies that work for you is important.

Take the time to practice the techniques we've discussed, and don't hesitate to seek support when you need it. You have the strength to manage your emotions and use them to your advantage. Keep exploring, reflecting, and growing Supergirl. You're on your way to becoming a true master of your feelings!

Chapter Four

Sharpening Communication Skills

Communication is one of the most important skills you can develop. It's the key to building strong relationships, solving problems, and expressing ideas and feelings. This section will explore how you can sharpen your communication skills. We'll explore how to express yourself clearly and listen empathetically. Let's get started!

Expressing Yourself Clearly

Why Clear Communication Matters

Clear communication helps you convey your thoughts, ideas, and feelings in a way that others can understand. Whether you're talking to a friend, a teacher, or a family member, expressing yourself is crucial.

Components of Clear Communication

Clarity: Make sure your message is easy to understand. Avoid using vague or confusing language.

Conciseness: Keep your message brief and to the point. Avoid unnecessary details that might distract from your main point.

Confidence: Speak with confidence. Believe in what you're saying and convey that belief through your tone and body language.

Respect: Show respect for the person you're communicating with. Be polite and considerate of their feelings and perspectives.

Tips for Expressing Yourself Clearly

Think Before You Speak

Before you start speaking, take a moment to gather your thoughts. Think about what you want to say and how you want to say it. This can help you communicate more effectively and avoid saying something you might regret later.

Use Simple Language

Using simple, straightforward language makes it easier for others to understand you. Avoid using jargon or complex words that might confuse your listener. If you need to use a technical term, explain it.

Be Specific

Be specific about what you're talking about. Instead of saying, "I'm upset," explain why you're upset. For example, "I'm upset because I felt left out when you didn't invite me to the party." Specificity helps the other person understand your perspective better.

Stay on Topic

Stay focused on the main point you want to communicate. Avoid going off on tangents or bringing up unrelated issues. If you need to discuss multiple topics, address them one at a time.

Use "I" Statements

Using "I" statements can help you express your feelings without sounding accusatory. Instead of saying, "You never listen to me," say, "I feel unheard when I'm not listened to." This shifts the focus to your feelings and makes the conversation less confrontational.

Pay Attention to Nonverbal Cues

Your body language, facial expressions, and tone of voice all play a role in communication. Make sure your nonverbal cues match your words. For example, if you're apologizing, ensure your tone is sincere, and your body language shows remorse.

Ask for Feedback

After expressing yourself, ask the other person if they understood you. This allows them to clarify any misinformation and shows that you value their perspective.

Practicing Clear Communication

Role-Playing

Role-playing can be a fun and effective way to practice clear communication. You can do this with a friend or family member. Take turns being the speaker and the listener. Choose different scenarios, such as discussing a school project or resolving a conflict, and practice expressing yourself clearly.

Recording Yourself

Record yourself speaking about a topic for a few minutes. Then, listen to the recording and evaluate how clear your communication was. Did you stay on topic? Were your points clear and concise? This can help you identify areas for improvement.

Public Speaking

Public speaking is a great way to build your communication skills and confidence. Look for opportunities to speak in front of a group, such as giving a presentation at school or participating in a debate. The more you practice, the more comfortable you'll become.

Writing Practice

Writing can help you organize your thoughts and practice transparent communication. Write about a topic you're passionate about, and then read it aloud to see how it sounds. This can help you improve both your writing and speaking skills.

Handling Difficult Conversations

Sometimes, you must have difficult conversations, such as resolving conflicts or delivering bad news. Here are some tips to help you handle these conversations with clarity and respect:

Stay Calm

It's important to stay calm during difficult conversations. Take deep breaths and remind yourself to focus on the issue. Keeping your emotions in check can help you communicate more effectively.

Be Honest

Be honest about your feelings and perspectives. Avoid sugarcoating or hiding the truth, as this can lead to misinformation. But be mindful of how you deliver the message to avoid hurting the other person's feelings.

Listen Actively

Active listening is crucial during difficult conversations. Listen to the other person's perspective and show that you understand them. This can help de-escalate tension and build mutual respect.

Find Common Ground

Look for areas of agreement and build on them. Finding common ground can help you work towards a resolution and make the conversation more productive.

Stay Solution-Oriented

Focus on finding a solution rather than dwelling on the problem. Discuss possible ways to resolve the issue and agree on an action plan. This can help you move forward and maintain a positive relationship.

Real-Life Examples of Clear Communication

To inspire you further, let's look at some real-life examples of clear communication:

1. **Malala Yousafzai**: Malala is a strong advocate for girls' education. Her speeches are clear, concise, and passionate. She uses simple language to convey her message and connect with her audience. Her ability to communicate has inspired millions around the world.

2. **Greta Thunberg**: Greta is a young climate activist known for her straightforward and impactful speeches. She clearly articulates her message about the urgency of addressing climate change, and her clear communication has mobilized young people worldwide to act.

3. **Emma Watson**: Emma is an actress and advocate for gender equality. Her speeches, such as her famous HeForShe campaign speech, are well-organized and articulate. She uses personal stories and specific examples to make her points clear and relatable.

These individuals demonstrate the power of clear communication to make a positive impact. You can become a more effective communicator by following their example and practicing the tips we've discussed.

Listening with Empathy

Listening is just as essential as speaking in communication. Listening with empathy means knowing and sharing another person's feelings. It's about putting yourself in their shoes and seeing things from their perspective. Empathetic listening builds trust, strengthens relationships, and helps resolve conflicts.

Why Empathetic Listening Matters

1. **Builds Trust**: When you listen empathetically, you show that you care about the other person's feelings and experiences. This builds trust and strengthens your relationship.

2. **Improves Understanding**: Empathetic listening helps you understand the other person's perspective. This can lead to better communication and problem-solving.

3. **Reduces Conflict**: When people feel heard and understood, they're less likely to become defensive or angry. This can help prevent or resolve conflicts.

4. **Improves Emotional Support**: Empathetic listening

provides emotional support. It shows that you're there for the other person and willing to help them through their challenges.

Components of Empathetic Listening

1. **Presence**: Be fully present in the moment. Give the other person your undivided attention.

2. **Understanding**: Seek to understand the other person's feelings and perspective.

3. **Non-judgmental**: Listen without judging or interrupting.

4. **Compassion**: Show compassion and empathy for the other person's experiences.

Tips for Listening with Empathy

Give Your Full Attention

When someone is speaking to you, could you give them your full attention? Put away distractions like your phone or other devices. Make eye contact and show that you focus on what they're saying.

Show That You're Listening

Use nonverbal cues to show that you're listening. Nod your head, smile, and use appropriate facial expressions. These signals let the speaker know that you're engaged and interested.

Reflect Back

Reflect on what the other person has said to show that you understand. For example, you might say, "It sounds like you're feeling frustrated because your project didn't turn out as planned." This shows that you're listening and helps clarify any misinformation.

Ask Open-Ended Questions

Ask open-ended questions to encourage the speaker to share more. Open-ended questions can't be answered with a simple "yes" or "no." For example, "Can you tell me more about what happened?" or "How did that make you feel?"

Validate Their Feelings

Validation means acknowledging and accepting the other person's feelings. You might say, "I can see why you would feel that way," or "That sounds tough." Validation shows that you respect their emotions and experiences.

Avoid Interrupting

Let the other person speak without interruption. Interrupting can make them feel unheard of and disrespected. Wait until they've finished speaking before you respond.

Be Patient

Sometimes, people need time to express their thoughts and feelings. Be patient and give them the space they need to share. Avoid rushing them or finishing their sentences.

Offer Support

After listening empathetically, offer your support. This could be advice, a helping hand, or simply being there for them. Ask how you can help and respect their wishes.

Practicing Empathetic Listening

Active Listening Exercises

Practice active listening with a friend or family member. Take turns being the speaker and the listener. Focus on using the empathetic listening techniques we've discussed. Afterward, share feedback on how it felt and what you could improve.

Empathy Journaling

Keep a journal where you reflect on your interactions with others. Write about a recent conversation and how you practiced empathetic listening. Note what went well and what you could improve. This can help you become more aware of your listening habits and develop your skills.

Role-Playing

Role-playing can be a fun way to practice empathetic listening. Create different scenarios, such as comforting an upset friend or discussing a conflict with a family member. Practice listening with empathy and providing support.

Mindfulness Meditation

Mindfulness meditation can help you become more present and attentive. Focus on your breath and let go of distractions. This can improve your ability to be present and listen empathetically in conversations.

Overcoming Challenges in Empathetic Listening

Dealing with Distractions

Distractions are everywhere in our busy lives. To be an empathetic listener, minimize distractions as much as possible. Find a quiet place to talk and put away devices that might interrupt your focus.

Managing Your Emotions

Sometimes, listening to someone else's problems can trigger your own emotions. It is essential to manage your feelings and stay focused on the other person. Take deep breaths and remind yourself to stay present. If necessary, take a break and return to the conversation when you feel calmer.

Avoiding Judgment

We all have opinions and perspectives, but empathetic listening requires putting those aside. Avoid judging the other person's feelings or experiences. Instead, focus on knowing and validating their perspective.

Balancing Empathy and Boundaries

Although being empathetic is important, maintaining healthy boundaries is also essential. If you're feeling overwhelmed or drained, taking a step back is okay. Let the other person know you care and will be there for them, but also take care of your well-being.

Real-Life Examples of Empathetic Listening

Let's look at some real-life examples of empathetic listening:

1. **Fred Rogers**: Fred Rogers, the beloved host of "Mister Rogers' Neighborhood," was known for his empathetic listening skills. He listened to children with patience and compassion, validating their feelings and providing a safe space for them to express themselves. His empathetic listening helped millions of children feel understood and supported.

2. **Oprah Winfrey**: Oprah Winfrey is a renowned talk show host and philanthropist known for her empathetic listening. She listens to her guests with genuine interest and compassion, asking thoughtful questions and validating their experiences. Her empathetic listening has helped countless individuals share their stories and find healing.

3. **Barack Obama**: Former President Barack Obama is praised for his empathetic listening skills. He often took the time to listen to people's concerns and perspectives, showing genuine empathy and knowledge. His empathetic listening helped build trust and foster positive relationships.

These individuals demonstrate the strength of empathetic listening in building connections and making a positive impact. You can become a more compassionate listener by following their example and practicing the tips we've discussed.

Sharpening your communication skills involves both expressing yourself clearly and listening with empathy. Clear communication helps you convey your thoughts and feelings effectively. In contrast, empathetic listening enables you to understand and connect with others. By practicing these skills, you can build stronger relationships, resolve conflicts, and confidently navigate life's challenges.

Remember, communication is a skill that takes time and effort to develop. Be patient with yourself, and keep practicing. The more you practice, the more confident and effective you'll become. Keep exploring, reflecting, and growing Supergirl. You have the strength to become an excellent communicator and positively impact the world!

CHAPTER FIVE

Building Strong Friendships and Relationships

Making New Friends

Hey there, Supergirl! Friendships are one of the most beautiful parts of life. This brings joy, support, and shared experiences that make life richer. But making new friends can sometimes feel scary, especially if you're shy or new to a place. Don't worry, though – everyone feels that way at times. Let's explore the exciting world of making new friends and nurturing connections.

Why Friendships Matter

Friends play a crucial role in our lives. They are our companions, cheerleaders, and confidants. Good friends can boost your happiness, improve self-confidence, and support you during tough times. Friendships teach you valuable life skills like empathy, cooperation, and communication. They also make everyday activities more fun and memorable.

Qualities of a Good Friend

Before we discuss how to make new friends, it's essential to understand what makes a good friend. Here are some qualities to look for in a friend and to cultivate in yourself:

1. Trustworthiness: A good friend is reliable and keeps their promises. They are someone you can trust with your secrets and feelings.

2. Loyalty: Good friends stand by you through thick and thin, supporting you even when times are tough.

3. Kindness: A kind friend is caring and compassionate. Show empathy and be considerate of your feelings.

4. Respect: Respectful friends value your opinions and boundaries. They treat you with dignity and expect the same in return.

5. Fun: A good friend makes you laugh and brings joy to your life. They enjoy spending time with you and sharing activities.

Steps to Making New Friends

Making new friends involves putting yourself out and being open to new experiences. Here are some steps to help you connect with others and build lasting friendships:

Be Open and Approachable

A friendly smile and open body language can make a big difference. People are likelier to feel comfortable talking to you when you appear approachable. Make eye contact, smile, and be mindful of your posture. Avoid crossing your arms or looking down at your phone when trying to make new friends.

Start Small

You don't have to explore deep conversations right away. Start with small talk to break the ice. Simple questions like "How was your weekend?" or "Do you like this class?" can initiate a conversation. Small talk can lead to more meaningful discussions as you get to know each other.

Find Common Interests

Shared interests are an excellent foundation for friendship. Think about the activities or hobbies you enjoy and look for opportunities to connect with others who share those interests. Join clubs, sports teams, or extracurricular activities where you can meet people with similar passions.

Be a Good Listener

Listening is a vital part of communication and building connections. Show genuine interest in what the other person is saying. Ask follow-up questions and respond thoughtfully. Being a good listener shows that you care and helps you understand the other person better.

Be Yourself

Authenticity is important in building genuine friendships. Be yourself and let your true personality shine. Trying to be someone you're not can lead to superficial connections. True friends will appreciate you for who you are.

Take Initiative

Sometimes, making new friends requires taking the first step. Feel free to initiate conversations or invite someone to join you for an activity. Let's meet for lunch, study together, or watch a movie. Taking the initiative shows that you're interested in getting to know them better.

Be Patient

Building friendships takes time. Don't get discouraged if you don't form instant connections. Keep putting yourself out there and be patient. With time, you'll find people who click with you and share your interests and values.

Overcoming Shyness

If you're naturally shy, making new friends might feel incredibly challenging. Here are some tips to help you overcome shyness and build your confidence:

Practice Self-Compassion

Be kind to yourself and recognize that it's okay to feel shy. Many people experience shyness, which doesn't define your ability to make friends. Treat yourself with the same kindness and knowing you would offer a friend.

Take Small Steps

Start with small, manageable steps to build your confidence. For example, practice making eye contact and smiling at people you pass in the hallway. Gradually work your way up to starting small conversations and joining group activities.

Prepare Topics

Having a few conversation topics in mind can help ease anxiety. Think about things you enjoy talking about or recent events you can discuss. Having a mental list of topics can boost your confidence when initiating conversations.

Join Supportive Environments

Look for environments where you feel safe and supported. Joining clubs or groups that focus on your interests can provide a sense of belonging and make it easier to connect with others. Supportive environments can help you feel more comfortable being yourself.

Celebrate Progress

Acknowledge and celebrate your progress, no matter how small. Each step you take towards overcoming shyness is an achievement. Reward yourself for your efforts and remind yourself that you're growing and improving.

Dealing with Rejection

Rejection is a natural part of life and can happen when making new friends. It's essential not to take it personally and to keep a positive mindset. Here are some tips for dealing with rejection:

Stay Positive

Remember that rejection doesn't define your worth. It simply means that the connection wasn't the right fit. Stay positive and keep looking for opportunities to meet new people. Focus on the friendships you already have and continue to build those connections.

Learn from the Experience

Reflect on the experience and consider if there's anything you can learn from it. Did you notice any areas where you can improve your communication skills? Use rejection as an opportunity for growth and self-improvement.

Keep Trying

Don't let rejection discourage you from trying again. Making new friends takes effort and persistence. Keep putting yourself out there and stay open to new experiences. With time, you'll find people who appreciate and value your friendship.

Practicing Friendship Skills

Building solid friendships requires practice and effort. Here are some activities to help you practice your friendship skills:

Role-Playing

Role-playing can be a fun way to practice making new friends. Pair up with a friend or family member and take turns being the new person and the one initiating the conversation. Practice different scenarios, such as introducing yourself, starting a conversation, and inviting someone to join an activity.

Group Activities

Participate in group activities to meet new people and practice your social skills. Join clubs, sports teams, or community events. Group activities provide a relaxed setting for making connections and building friendships.

Volunteer Work

Volunteering is a great way to meet new people and positively impact your community. Look for volunteer opportunities that align with your interests. Working together for a common cause can help you form meaningful connections with others.

Social Events

Attend social events like parties, school dances, or community gatherings. These events provide opportunities to meet new people in a fun and relaxed environment. Be open to starting conversations and getting to know others.

Real-Life Examples of Making Friends

To inspire you further, let's look at some real-life examples of people who have successfully made new friends:

1. **Malala Yousafzai**: Despite facing significant challenges, Malala has built strong friendships through her advocacy work for girls' education. Her passion for the cause has connected her with like-minded individuals and created lasting bonds.

2. **J.K. Rowling**: The famous author of the Harry Potter series has spoken about the importance of friendships in her life. Rowling has built strong connections with fellow writers and fans, forming a supportive community that shares her love for storytelling.

3. **Emma Watson**: As a well-known actress and advocate for gender equality, Emma Watson has made friends through her activism and professional work. Her genuine and compassionate approach has helped her form meaningful relationships with people who share her values.

These individuals demonstrate that making new friends is possible, even in challenging circumstances. You can build strong and lasting friendships by following their example and practicing the tips we discussed.

Nurturing Connections

Once you've made new friends, nurturing those connections is essential. Building and maintaining solid friendships requires effort, communication, and mutual respect. Let's explore how to nurture your friendships and create lasting bonds.

Why Nurturing Friendships Matters

Nurturing friendships is essential for maintaining strong and healthy relationships. It helps deepen your connection with others, builds trust, and ensures your friendships last over time. Nurtured friendships provide emotional support, joy, and a sense of belonging.

Ways to Nurture Friendships

Stay Connected

Regular communication is vital to nurturing friendships. Stay in touch with your friends through texts, phone calls, or social media. Check-in on them, share updates about your life, and show that you care.

Spend Quality Time Together

Spending quality time together strengthens your bond and creates shared memories. Plan activities you enjoy, such as going to the movies, having a picnic, or playing sports. Quality time doesn't have to be extravagant – the connection matters.

Show Appreciation

Expressing gratitude and appreciation is important in any relationship. Let your friends know how much you value them and what you appreciate about them. Simple gestures like saying "thank you," giving compliments, or writing a heartfelt note can go a long way.

Be Supportive

Support your friends through both good times and bad. Celebrate their achievements and offer a listening ear when they're facing challenges. Show empathy and be there for them when they need you. Your support helps build trust and strengthens your friendship.

Communicate Openly

Open and honest communication is crucial for maintaining substantial friendships. Share your thoughts, feelings, and concerns with your friends, and please encourage them to do the same. Address any issues or misinformation calmly and respectfully.

Respect Boundaries

Respecting your friends' boundaries is essential for a healthy relationship. Understand their limits and be mindful of their needs.

If your friend needs space or time alone, respect their wishes and let them know you're there for them when they're ready.

Resolve Conflicts

Conflicts are a natural part of any relationship. When conflicts arise, address them calmly and constructively. Listen to each other's perspectives, find common ground, and work together to find a solution. Resolving conflicts strengthens your bond and helps you grow together.

Celebrate Together

Celebrate special occasions and milestones with your friends. Whether it's a birthday, graduation, or personal achievement, please try to celebrate their successes. Sharing in each other's joy creates positive memories and reinforces your connection.

Activities to Strengthen Friendships

Here are some fun and meaningful activities to help you nurture your friendships:

Friendship Journal

Start a friendship journal with your friend in which you both write about your experiences, thoughts, and feelings. This can be a creative way to stay connected and better understand each other. You can also include drawings, photos, and mementos.

Adventure Day

Plan an adventure day where you and your friend try something new together. It could be exploring a new hiking trail, visiting a museum, or trying a new hobby. Shared adventures create lasting memories and strengthen your bond.

Volunteer Together

Volunteering together can be a rewarding way to strengthen your friendship. Find a cause you both care about and volunteer your time and effort. Working together for a common goal fosters teamwork and deepens your connection.

Movie Night

Host a movie night to watch your favorite films or discover new ones. Make it cozy with blankets, popcorn, and snacks. Movie nights provide a relaxed setting for spending quality time together.

Cook or Bake Together

Cooking or baking together can be a fun and bonding experience. Choose a recipe you want to try and work together to create a delicious meal or treat. Enjoying the fruits of your labor together adds to the enjoyment.

Game Night

Plan a game night with board, card, or video games. Friendly competition and laughter make for a great time, and game nights are an excellent way to connect and have fun.

DIY Projects

Work on DIY projects or crafts together. Whether it's making friendship bracelets, painting, or building something, creative projects provide an opportunity for collaboration and creativity.

Study Sessions

Organize study sessions if you and your friend are in the same class or have similar academic goals. Studying together can be motivating and productive. You can help each other with complex subjects and celebrate your progress.

Real-Life Examples of Nurturing Friendships

To inspire you further, let's look at some real-life examples of people who have successfully nurtured their friendships:

1. **Taylor Swift and Selena Gomez**: These famous singers have maintained a strong friendship. They support each other's careers, celebrate successes, and spend quality time together. Their friendship is built on mutual respect, trust, and shared experiences.

2. **Michelle Obama and Oprah Winfrey**: Former First Lady Michelle Obama and media mogul Oprah Winfrey share

a deep and lasting friendship. They support each other's endeavors, offer emotional support, and publicly celebrate their achievements. Their friendship is a testament to the strength of mutual respect and admiration.

3. **Matt Damon and Ben Affleck**: These actors and childhood friends have maintained a close friendship throughout their careers. They've collaborated on projects, supported each other during challenging times, and celebrated each other's successes. Their friendship demonstrates the importance of loyalty and support.

These individuals demonstrate that nurturing friendships requires effort, communication, and mutual respect. You can build and maintain strong and lasting friendships by following their example and practicing our discussed tips.

Building solid friendships and relationships is a rewarding and enriching part of life. By making new friends and nurturing your connections, you can create a supportive network of people who bring joy, comfort, and companionship into your life.

Making and nurturing friendships takes effort, patience, and genuine care. Be open, approachable, and authentic. Show appreciation, support, and respect for your friends. Communicate openly and address conflicts constructively. Celebrate each other's successes and create lasting memories together.

With these skills and practices, you can build and maintain strong, meaningful friendships that will enrich your life and bring you happiness. Keep exploring, connecting, and growing Supergirl. The world is full of wonderful people waiting to be your friends!

CHAPTER SIX

Hygiene and Self-Care Tips

Daily Routines

Hey, Supergirl! Taking care of your body and mind is essential for your overall well-being. Good hygiene and self-care routines not only keep you healthy but also boost your confidence and happiness. Let's explore essential hygiene and self-care tips to help you stay healthy and happy.

Why Daily Routines Matter

Establishing a daily routine ensures consistency in your hygiene and self-care practices. It helps prevent health issues and promotes a sense of structure and stability, nurturing both your physical and mental well-being.

Morning Routine

Starting your day with a consistent morning routine sets a positive tone. Here's a step-by-step guide to creating a morning routine that works for you:

1. **Wake Up Early:** Waking up early gives you enough time to complete your morning routine without feeling rushed. Aim to wake up at the same time every day, even on weekends, to maintain a consistent sleep schedule.

2. **Hydrate:** Your body needs hydration after a night's sleep. Drink a glass of water when you wake up to kickstart your metabolism and rehydrate. Adding a slice of lemon to your water can provide a refreshing boost of vitamin C.

3. **Brush Your Teeth:** Brushing your teeth twice a day is crucial for good oral hygiene. Use a fluoride toothpaste and a soft-bristled toothbrush. Brush for at least two minutes, reaching all areas of your mouth, including your tongue and gums. Flossing once a day helps remove plaque and food particles between your teeth.

4. **Wash Your Face:** Washing your face in the morning helps remove any dirt, oil, and sweat accumulated overnight. Use a gentle facial cleanser suitable for your skin type. Rinse with lukewarm water and pat your face dry with a clean towel. Follow up with a moisturizer to keep your skin hydrated.

5. **Shower:** Showering in the morning can help wake you up and prepare you for the day ahead. Use a mild soap or body wash to cleanse your skin. Pay attention to areas that tend to sweat more, such as your underarms, groin, and feet. Rinse thoroughly and dry off with a clean towel.

6. **Apply Deodorant:** Deodorant helps control body odor and keeps you feeling fresh throughout the day. Choose a deodorant that works for you and apply it to clean, dry skin after your shower.

7. **Style Your Hair:** Take a few minutes to style your hair in a way that makes you feel confident and comfortable. Whether brushing, combing, or styling with accessories, taking care of your hair can boost your self-esteem.

8. **Eat a Healthy Breakfast:** Breakfast is the most important meal of the day. Fuel your body with a nutritious breakfast that balances protein, carbohydrates, and healthy fats. Some healthy breakfast options include oatmeal with fruits and nuts, whole-grain toast with avocado and eggs, Greek yogurt with berries and granola, and smoothies with spinach, banana, and almond milk.

9. **Plan Your Day:** Take a few minutes to plan your day. Review your schedule, set priorities, and make a to-do list. Planning helps you stay organized and focused, reducing stress and improving productivity.

Evening Routine

An evening routine helps you wind down and prepare for a restful night's sleep. Here's a step-by-step guide to creating an evening routine that promotes relaxation and good hygiene:

1. **Unwind:** Take some time to relax after a busy day. Engage in activities that help you de-stress, such as reading a book, listening to music, or practicing mindfulness.

2. **Skincare:** Caring for your skin at night is essential for maintaining a healthy complexion. Follow these steps: Cleanse: Remove makeup and cleanse your face to remove dirt, oil, and impurities. Tone: Use a toner to balance your skin's pH levels and prepare it for moisturizing. Moisturize: Apply a night cream or moisturizer to hydrate and nourish your skin.

3. **Brush Your Teeth:** Brushing your teeth before bed helps remove food particles and plaque that can cause cavities and gum disease. Remember to floss and rinse with mouthwash for a thorough clean.

4. **Shower or Bath:** A warm shower or bath in the evening can help relax your muscles and prepare you for sleep. To improve relaxation, use calming scents like lavender or chamomile.

5. **Prepare for Tomorrow:** Lay out your clothes and pack your bag for the next day. Preparing in advance can save you time and reduce morning stress.

6. **Reflect and Journal:** Spend a few minutes reflecting on your day. Write down your thoughts, accomplishments, and any challenges you faced. Journaling can help you process your emotions and set positive intentions for the next day.

7. **Sleep Routine:** Establishing a consistent sleep routine is crucial for good health. Aim to go to bed at the same time every night and wake up at the same time every morning. Create a relaxing bedtime environment by dimming the lights, turning off electronic devices, and practicing calming activities like deep breathing or meditation.

Weekly Hygiene Routine

In addition to your daily routine, certain hygiene practices should be done weekly to maintain overall cleanliness and health. Here are some essential weekly hygiene tips:

1. **Change Your Sheets and Towels:** Regularly changing your bed sheets and towels helps prevent the buildup of bacteria and allergens. Aim to change your sheets and pillowcases once a week and your towels every three to four days.

2. **Clean Your Makeup Brushes:** Makeup brushes can harbor bacteria, oil, and product buildup. Clean your makeup brushes once a week with a gentle cleanser or a brush-cleaning solution. Rinse thoroughly and let them air dry.

3. **Groom Your Nails:** Trim and file your nails regularly to keep them neat and prevent breakage. Clean under your nails to remove dirt and bacteria. Consider applying a moisturizing cuticle cream to keep your cuticles healthy.

4. **Deep Clean Your Hair:** In addition to regular washing, deep clean your hair weekly with a clarifying shampoo to remove product buildup and excess oil. Follow up with a deep conditioning treatment to nourish and hydrate your hair.

5. **Exfoliate Your Skin:** Exfoliating your skin once a week helps remove dead skin cells and promotes a healthy, glowing complexion. Use a gentle exfoliator suitable for your skin type and follow up with a moisturizer.

Staying Healthy and Happy

Good hygiene and self-care are essential for overall health and happiness. Taking care of your physical and mental well-being helps you feel your best and live a balanced life. Let's explore some essential tips for staying healthy and happy.

Physical Health

1. **Nutrition:** Eating a balanced diet is essential for maintaining good health. Aim to include a variety of nutrient-dense foods in your diet, such as:

   ○ **Fruits and Vegetables:** Rich in vitamins, minerals, and antioxidants.

   ○ **Whole Grains:** Provide fiber, vitamins, and minerals.

   ○ **Lean Proteins:** Include sources like chicken, fish, beans, and nuts.

   ○ **Dairy or Dairy Alternatives:** Provide calcium and vitamin D for bone health.

   ○ **Healthy Fats:** Include sources like avocados, nuts, seeds, and olive oil.

2. **Exercise:** Regular physical activity is crucial for maintaining physical health and mental well-being. Aim for at least 60 minutes of moderate to vigorous exercise each day. Here are some fun and effective ways to stay active:

   ○ **Dancing:** Join a dance class or dance along to your favorite music at home.

   ○ **Sports:** Participate in team sports like soccer, basketball, or volleyball.

- **Walking or Running:** Go for a walk or run in your neighborhood or at a local park.

- **Yoga:** Practice yoga to improve flexibility, strength, and relaxation.

- **Cycling:** Ride your bike around your neighborhood or on designated trails.

3. **Sleep:** Getting enough sleep is vital for overall health and well-being. Aim for 8-10 hours of sleep each night. Establish a consistent sleep schedule and create a relaxing bedtime routine to promote restful sleep.

4. **Hydration:** Staying hydrated is essential for maintaining good health. Drink plenty of water throughout the day, especially after physical activity. Carry a reusable water bottle with you to remind yourself to stay hydrated.

5. **Regular Check-Ups:** Regular medical check-ups and dental visits are essential for maintaining your health. Schedule annual physical exams, dental cleanings, and eye exams. Don't hesitate to seek medical advice if you have any health concerns.

Mental Health

1. **Stress Management:** Managing stress is crucial for maintaining mental well-being. Here are some effective stress management techniques:

   - **Deep Breathing:** Practice breathing exercises to calm your mind and body.

   - **Mindfulness and Meditation:** Practice mindfulness and meditation to stay present and focused.

   - **Exercise:** Physical activity helps reduce stress and improve mood.

   - **Hobbies:** Engage in activities you enjoy to relax and unwind.

   - **Social Support:** Spend time with friends and family who provide emotional support.

2. **Positive Thinking:** Cultivating a positive mindset can improve your mental well-being. Practice positive thinking by:

   - **Gratitude:** Keep a gratitude journal and write what you're thankful for daily.

   - **Affirmations:** Use positive affirmations to boost your confidence and self-esteem.

   - **Reframing:** Challenge negative thoughts and reframe

them in a positive light.

3. **Emotional Expression:** Expressing your emotions is essential for mental health. Find healthy ways to express your feelings, such as:

   ○ **Journaling:** Write about your thoughts and emotions in a journal.

   ○ **Talking:** Share your feelings with a trusted friend or family member.

   ○ **Creative Outlets:** Use creative activities like drawing, painting, or music to express emotions.

4. **Healthy Boundaries:** Setting and maintaining healthy boundaries is necessary for mental well-being. Learn to say no when you need to and prioritize self-care. Respect your limits and communicate them to others.

5. **Self-Compassion:** Practice self-compassion by treating yourself with kindness and understanding. Avoid self-criticism and acknowledge your efforts and achievements. Celebrate your strengths and be gentle with yourself during challenging times.

Building Healthy Habits

Developing healthy habits takes time and consistency. Here are some tips to help you build and maintain healthy habits:

1. **Set Realistic Goals:** Set achievable and realistic goals for your health and well-being. Break down larger goals into smaller, manageable steps. Celebrate your progress along the way.

2. **Create a Routine:** Establish a daily routine that includes time for hygiene, self-care, and healthy activities. Consistency is critical to building lasting habits.

3. **Track Your Progress:** Track your progress using a journal, planner, or app. Recording your achievements and challenges can help you stay motivated and accountable.

4. **Find a Support System:** Surround yourself with supportive friends and family who encourage your healthy habits. Share your goals with them and seek their support when needed.

5. **Stay Flexible:** Be flexible and adaptable in your approach to healthy habits. Life can be unpredictable, and adjusting your routine when necessary is okay. The key is to stay committed to your overall goals.

Good hygiene and self-care are essential for maintaining your physical and mental health. By establishing daily routines and incorporating healthy habits, you can take control of your well-being and feel your best every day.

Remember, taking care of yourself is a lifelong journey. Be patient with yourself and celebrate your progress. Stay consistent with your routines and make self-care a priority. Supergirl, you have the strength to create a healthy, happy, and balanced life!

CHAPTER SEVEN

Growth Mindset for Success

Embracing Challenges

Hello, Supergirl! Success isn't just about natural talent or intelligence. It's about how you approach challenges and setbacks. Cultivating a growth mindset is crucial for success in every area of your life. A growth mindset helps you see challenges as opportunities to learn and grow rather than obstacles to avoid. Let's explore how you can embrace challenges and turn them into stepping stones for success.

What is a Growth Mindset?

A growth mindset is the belief that your abilities and intelligence can be developed through effort, learning, and perseverance. It's about seeing the potential for improvement in every experience and being open to learning new things. This contrasts with a fixed mindset, where people believe their abilities are static and cannot be changed.

Why Embrace Challenges?

Challenges are an inevitable part of life. Embracing rather than avoiding them helps you develop resilience, creativity, and problem-solving skills. Here's why you should welcome challenges:

- **Growth and Improvement:** Challenges push you out of your comfort zone and help you develop new skills and knowledge.

- **Increased Confidence:** Overcoming challenges boosts your self-esteem and confidence in your abilities.

- **Problem-Solving Skills:** Facing challenges teaches you to think critically and develop creative solutions.

- **Resilience:** Each challenge you overcome makes you stronger and more resilient, better prepared for future obstacles.

How to Embrace Challenges

1. **Change Your Perspective:** Start by changing how you view challenges. Instead of seeing them as threats or insurmountable obstacles, see them as opportunities to learn and grow. Remind yourself that every challenge is a

chance to become better and stronger.

2. **Set Realistic Goals:** Break down larger challenges into smaller, manageable goals. This will make them less overwhelming and give you a clear path. Celebrate each small victory along the way to stay motivated.

3. **Stay Positive:** Maintain a positive attitude when facing challenges. Focus on what you can learn from the experience rather than what could go wrong. Positive thinking can boost your motivation and resilience.

4. **Seek Support:** Don't hesitate to ask for help when facing a challenge. Seek support from friends, family, teachers, or mentors. They can offer advice, encouragement, and different perspectives to help you overcome obstacles.

5. **Practice Perseverance:** Perseverance is key to overcoming challenges. Keep pushing forward, even when things get tough. Remember that setbacks are a normal part of the process. Stay committed to your goals and don't give up.

6. **Learn from Failure:** Failure is a natural part of embracing challenges. Instead of fearing failure, see it as a learning opportunity. Reflect on what went wrong, what you can learn from the experience, and how to improve next time. Every failure brings you one step closer to success.

Examples of Embracing Challenges

1. **Thomas Edison:** The inventor of the light bulb faced numerous challenges and failures in his experiments. He viewed each failure as a step closer to success and famously said, "I have not failed. I've just found 10,000 ways that won't work."

2. **J.K. Rowling:** The author of the Harry Potter series faced many rejections from publishers before her books became a global success. She embraced the challenges and persisted in her writing, eventually becoming one of the most successful authors in the world.

3. **Michael Jordan:** Widely regarded as one of the greatest basketball players of all time, Michael Jordan faced many challenges throughout his career. He was cut from his high school basketball team but used this setback to motivate him to work harder and improve his skills.

These individuals demonstrate that embracing challenges is crucial for achieving success. Adopting a growth mindset and persevering through obstacles, you can overcome challenges and reach your goals.

Learning from Mistakes

Mistakes are a natural and valuable part of the learning process. They provide opportunities for growth, improvement, and self-discovery. Let's explore how you can learn from your mistakes and use them to cultivate a growth mindset for success.

Why Mistakes Matter

Mistakes are essential for several reasons:

- **Learning Opportunities:** Mistakes help you identify areas to improve and develop new skills.

- **Personal Growth:** Learning from errors fosters personal growth and self-awareness.

- **Resilience:** Overcoming mistakes builds resilience and the ability to bounce back from setbacks.

- **Innovation:** Mistakes can lead to new ideas and innovations by encouraging creative problem-solving.

How to Learn from Mistakes

1. **Acknowledge Your Mistakes:** The first step in learning from mistakes is acknowledging them. Take responsibility for your actions and recognize what went wrong. Avoid blaming others or making excuses. Accepting your mistakes is crucial for personal growth and improvement.

2. **Reflect on the Experience:** Take time to reflect on the mistake and what you can learn from it. Ask yourself questions like: What caused the mistake? What could I have done differently? What did I learn from this experience? Reflecting on your mistakes helps you gain valuable insights and avoid repeating them in the future.

3. **Seek Feedback:** Feedback from others can provide valuable perspectives on your mistakes. Ask for constructive feedback from trusted friends, family members, teachers, or mentors. They can offer advice and suggestions for improvement.

4. **Plan for Improvement:** Based on your reflections and feedback, create an improvement plan. Identify specific steps you can take to avoid making the same mistake again. Set realistic goals and develop an action plan to achieve them.

5. **Practice Self-Compassion:** It's important to be kind to yourself when you make mistakes. Avoid harsh self-criticism and practice self-compassion. Treat yourself with the same kindness and encouragement you would offer a friend. Everyone makes mistakes, and they are a natural part of the learning process.

6. **Stay Persistent:** Learning from mistakes requires persistence and determination. Keep trying, even if you encounter setbacks along the way. Stay committed to your goals and continue to work towards improvement.

Examples of Learning from Mistakes

1. **Albert Einstein:** The famous physicist struggled in school and was even considered a slow learner by his teachers. Despite these setbacks, he persevered and went on to develop the theory of relativity, one of the most important scientific discoveries of all time.

2. **Steve Jobs:** The co-founder of Apple Inc. faced numerous failures and setbacks throughout his career. He was even fired from his own company. However, he learned from these experiences, returned to Apple, and led the company to unprecedented success.

3. **Oprah Winfrey:** The media mogul faced many challenges and mistakes early in her career, including being fired from her first television job. She used these experiences to learn and grow, eventually building a media empire and becoming one of the most influential women in the world.

These individuals show that mistakes are valuable learning opportunities. By acknowledging and learning from their mistakes, they achieved great success. You, too, can learn from your mistakes and use them as stepping stones to success.

Developing a Growth Mindset

Changing your thoughts about challenges, mistakes, and effort is essential to cultivate a growth mindset. Here are some tips to help you develop a growth mindset:

1. **Embrace the Process:** Focus on the learning process rather than the result. Understand that growth and improvement take time and effort. Celebrate your progress and the small steps you take toward your goals.

2. **Value Effort:** Recognize the importance of effort in achieving success. Understand that hard work, perseverance, and dedication are crucial for growth and improvement. Value the effort you put into your work, even if the results aren't perfect.

3. **Celebrate Learning:** Celebrate the learning that comes from challenges and mistakes. View every experience as an opportunity to learn and grow. Acknowledge the lessons you've learned and the skills you've developed.

4. **Stay Curious:** Cultivate a sense of curiosity and a love for learning. Be open to new experiences, ideas, and perspectives. Stay curious and explore new opportunities for growth and improvement.

5. **Surround Yourself with Support:** Surround yourself with people who support your growth and encourage a growth mindset. Seek out friends, mentors, and role models who inspire you and help you stay motivated.

6. **Practice Gratitude:** Gratitude can help you maintain a positive mindset and focus on the positive aspects of your experiences. Keep a gratitude journal and write down things you're grateful for daily. Reflect on the lessons you've learned and the progress you've made.

Activities to Cultivate a Growth Mindset

Here are some activities to help you develop and strengthen your growth mindset:

1. **Growth Mindset Journal:** Keep a growth mindset journal where you write about your challenges, mistakes, and learning experiences. Reflect on what you've learned from each experience and how you can apply those lessons in the future.

2. **Mindset Affirmations:** Use positive affirmations to reinforce your growth mindset. Write down affirmations like "I am capable of learning and growing," "Challenges help me become stronger," and "Mistakes are opportunities to learn." Repeat these affirmations daily to boost your confidence and motivation.

3. **Mindset Visualization:** Visualize yourself embracing challenges and learning from mistakes. Think about how you'll feel and what you'll achieve by adopting a growth mindset. Visualization can help you stay focused and

motivated.

4. **Growth Mindset Quotes:** Create a collection of growth mindset quotes that inspire and motivate you. Write them on sticky notes and place them around your room or workspace. Here are a few to get you started:

   - "The only way to achieve the impossible is to believe it is possible." – Charles Kingsleigh

   - "Success is not final, failure is not fatal: It is the courage to continue that count." – Winston Churchill

   - "I can accept failure; everyone fails at something. But I can't accept not trying." – Michael Jordan

5. **Challenge Yourself:** Set a goal to try something new or do a challenging task weekly. Embrace the discomfort and uncertainty that come with new experiences. Reflect on what you've learned and how you've grown from each challenge.

Cultivating a growth mindset is key to achieving success and personal growth. By embracing challenges and learning from mistakes, you can develop resilience, creativity, and a love for learning. Remember, success isn't about being perfect or avoiding failure. It's about approaching challenges and using them as opportunities to learn and grow.

Stay curious, stay positive, and remain persistent, Supergirl. You have the strength to cultivate a growth mindset and achieve great things. Embrace the journey, celebrate your progress, and keep striving for improvement. The world is full of opportunities for growth and success – go out there and seize them!

CHAPTER EIGHT

Radiating Confidence

Standing Tall

Hello, Supergirl! Confidence is an incredible super strength. It helps you navigate challenges, pursue your dreams, and be your authentic self. Confidence isn't about being perfect; it's about believing in yourself and your abilities. This section will explore how to stand tall and confidently face your fears. Let's get started!

Why Confidence Matters

Confidence plays a vital role in your overall well-being and success. Here are a few reasons why confidence is necessary:

- **Improves Performance:** When you believe in yourself, you're more likely to perform well in school, sports, and other activities.

- **Enhances Relationships:** Confidence helps you communicate effectively, make new friends, and build strong relationships.

- **Boosts Resilience:** Confident people are better equipped to handle setbacks and bounce back from failures.

- **Promotes Happiness:** Confidence contributes to a positive self-image and overall happiness.

Standing Tall: Physical Confidence

Your body language can significantly impact your confidence levels. Standing tall isn't just about good posture but also about exuding confidence and self-assurance. Here's how you can use your body language to radiate confidence:

1. **Posture:** Good posture makes you look more confident and helps you feel more confident.

   - **Stand Up Straight:** Keep your shoulders back and your head held high. Think of a string pulling you up from the top of your head.

   - **Align Your Spine:** Your ears, shoulders, hips, and ankles should be in a straight line. Avoid slouching or leaning forward.

   - **Engage Your Core:** To support your lower back, keep

your abdominal muscles slightly engaged.

2. **Eye Contact:** Making eye contact is a solid way to show confidence. It demonstrates that you're engaged, attentive, and self-assured.

   ○ **Look People in the Eye:** When speaking to someone, maintain eye contact for a few seconds. Avoid staring, but don't look away too quickly.

   ○ **Practice with Friends:** If you're uncomfortable with eye contact, practice with friends or family. Gradually increase the duration of eye contact.

3. **Smiling:** A genuine smile can make you appear more approachable and confident. It also releases endorphins, which can boost your mood and confidence.

   ○ **Relax Your Face:** A tense or forced smile can look unnatural. Relax your facial muscles and let your smile reach your eyes.

   ○ **Smile Often:** Smile at people you pass by, during conversations, and even when alone. It will become more natural with practice.

4. **Body Language:** Your body language communicates a lot about your confidence.

- **Open Stance:** Stand with your feet shoulder-width apart and your arms relaxed at your sides. Avoid crossing your arms or legs, making you appear closed off.

- **Gestures:** Use natural hand gestures to emphasize your points during conversations. Avoid fidgeting or excessive movements.

- **Presence:** Take up space and avoid shrinking or making yourself smaller. Stand or sit with your back straight and your head held high.

Building Confidence from Within

Although body language is essential, true confidence comes from within. It's about believing in yourself and your abilities. Here are some strategies to build internal confidence:

1. **Positive Self-Talk:** The way you talk to yourself can significantly impact your confidence.

   - **Identify Negative Thoughts:** Listen to your inner dialogue and identify negative or self-critical thoughts.

   - **Challenge Negative Thoughts:** Ask yourself if these thoughts are accurate or helpful. Replace them with positive affirmations.

   - **Practice Daily:** Make positive self-talk a daily habit.

Repeat affirmations like "I am capable," "I am confident," and "I can achieve my goals."

2. **Set and Achieve Goals:** Setting and achieving goals can boost your confidence and give you a sense of accomplishment.

   ○ **SMART Goals:** Set goals that are Specific, Measurable, Achievable, Relevant, and Time-bound. For example, "I will improve my math grade by studying for 30 minutes daily for the next month."

   ○ **Break Down Goals:** Break larger goals into smaller, manageable steps. Celebrate each small achievement along the way.

   ○ **Stay Committed:** Stay focused and committed to your goals. Even though you face setbacks, keep moving forward.

3. **Embrace Your Strengths:** Recognizing and embracing your strengths can boost your self-esteem and confidence.

   ○ **Self-Reflection:** Take time to reflect on your strengths and accomplishments. Write them down in a journal.

   ○ **Seek Feedback:** Ask friends, family, and teachers about your strengths. This can provide valuable insights.

- **Celebrate Your Strengths:** Celebrate your unique qualities and talents. Use them to your advantage in different situations.

4. **Learn New Skills:** Learning new skills can expand your capabilities and boost your confidence.

- **Identify Interests:** Consider areas you're interested in or skills you'd like to develop. It could be anything from playing an instrument to learning a new language.

- **Take Action:** Enroll in classes, join clubs, or practice independently. Dedicate time and effort to learning and improving.

- **Embrace Challenges:** Don't be afraid to make mistakes or face challenges. Each step you take brings you closer to mastery.

5. **Practice Self-Care:** Taking care of your physical and mental well-being is crucial for building confidence.

- **Exercise:** Regular physical activity can boost your mood and energy levels. Find activities you enjoy, such as dancing, swimming, or hiking.

- **Healthy Eating:** Fuel your body with nutritious foods that provide energy and support overall health.

- **Rest:** Get enough sleep and take time to relax and unwind. Practice mindfulness or meditation to reduce stress.

- **Hobbies and Interests:** Engage in activities that bring joy and fulfillment. This can boost your overall well-being and confidence.

Facing Fears

Fear is natural but shouldn't keep you from pursuing your dreams and goals. Facing your fears is a solid way to build confidence and resilience. Here's how to confront and overcome your fears:

1. **Identify Your Fears:** The first step in overcoming fear is identifying what you're afraid of.

   - **Fear of Failure:** This fear can prevent you from trying new things or taking risks. It often involves worrying about making mistakes or not meeting expectations.

   - **Fear of Rejection:** This fear can make you hesitate to form new relationships or express your feelings. It involves worrying about being judged or not accepted by others.

   - **Fear of the Unknown:** This fear can make you avoid new experiences or changes. It involves worrying about what might happen or feeling uncertain about the future.

2. **Understand Your Fears:** Understanding the root cause of your fears can help you address them more effectively. Reflect on why you feel afraid and what triggers your anxiety. Consider how your fear impacts your life and what you might gain by overcoming it.

3. **Challenge Negative Thoughts:** Fear often involves negative thoughts and assumptions. Challenge these thoughts by questioning their validity and replacing them with positive, realistic ones.

   ○ **Identify Negative Thoughts:** Pay attention to the thoughts that arise when you feel afraid. Write them down if it helps.

   ○ **Question Their Validity:** Ask yourself if these thoughts are true or based on assumptions. Look for evidence to support or refute them.

   ○ **Replace with Positive Thoughts:** Replace negative thoughts with positive affirmations or realistic statements. For example, replace "I can't do this" with "I can learn and improve with practice."

4. **Take Small Steps:** Overcoming fear doesn't happen overnight. Start by taking small steps toward confronting your fear. Gradually increase the difficulty as you build confidence.

- **Set Achievable Goals:** Set small, manageable goals that challenge your fear. For example, if you lack confidence in public speaking, start by speaking in front of a small group of friends.

- **Practice Regularly:** Practice facing your fear regularly to build confidence and desensitize yourself. Consistent practice helps reduce anxiety over time.

- **Celebrate Progress:** Celebrate each small victory along the way. Acknowledge your progress and use it as motivation to keep going.

5. **Seek Support:** Facing your fears can be easier with the support of others. Seek support from friends, family, or a mentor. They can offer encouragement, advice, and a different perspective. Feel free to ask for help when you need it.

6. **Visualize Success:** Visualization is a powerful technique for overcoming fear. Imagine yourself successfully facing your fear and achieving your goals. Visualize the positive outcomes and how you'll feel once you've overcome your fear.

- **Find a Quiet Space:** Sit or lie in a quiet, comfortable space where you won't be disturbed.

- **Close Your Eyes:** Close your eyes and take a few deep

breaths to relax.

- **Visualize Success:** Imagine yourself in a situation where you're facing your fear. Visualize yourself feeling confident, calm, and successful. Focus on the positive emotions and outcomes.

7. **Practice Mindfulness:** Mindfulness can help you stay present and manage anxiety when facing your fears. Practice mindfulness techniques, such as deep breathing or meditation, to calm your mind and body.

- **Find a Comfortable Position:** Sit or lie down in a comfortable position.

- **Focus on Your Breath:** Close your eyes and focus on your breath. Notice the sensation of the air entering and leaving your body.

- **Stay Present:** When your mind wanders, gently bring your focus back to your breath. Practice this for a few minutes each day.

8. **Embrace Failure:** Failure is a natural part of facing your fears and pursuing your goals. Embrace failure as a learning opportunity and a step towards success. Remember that every successful person has faced failure along the way.

- **Reframe Failure:** Instead of seeing failure as a negative outcome, see it as a valuable learning experience. Ask yourself what you can learn from the situation and how to improve.

- ○ **Stay Persistent:** Don't let failure discourage you. Stay committed to your goals and keep trying. Each failure brings you one step closer to success.

- ○ **Celebrate Effort:** Celebrate the effort you put into facing your fear, regardless of the outcome. Recognize that taking action is a success in itself.

Examples of Facing Fears

1. **Rosa Parks:** Rosa Parks faced her fear of standing up against racial segregation when she refused to give up her seat on a bus. Her courageous act sparked the Civil Rights Movement and significantly changed American society.

2. **Malala Yousafzai:** Malala faced her fear of violence and persecution to advocate for girls' education in Pakistan. Even after being targeted by the Taliban, she continued her activism and became the youngest-ever Nobel Prize laureate.

3. **Bethany Hamilton:** After losing her arm in a shark attack, Bethany faced her fear of returning to surfing. She overcame her fear and became a professional surfer and an inspiration to many.

These individuals show that facing fears is essential for achieving greatness. They significantly impacted the world by confronting their fears and persevering through challenges. You, too, can overcome your fears and achieve your dreams.

Building a Confident Mindset

Developing a confident mindset to radiate confidence and face your fears is important. Here are some tips to help you build a confident mindset:

1. **Believe in Yourself:** Believe in your abilities and your growth potential. Trust that you have what it takes to achieve your goals and overcome challenges.

   - **Reflect on Past Successes:** Recall when you've succeeded or overcome challenges. Use these experiences as evidence of your capabilities.

   - **Set Realistic Expectations:** Set realistic and achievable goals. Celebrate your progress and accomplishments along the way.

   - **Surround Yourself with Positivity:** Surround yourself with people who support and believe in you. Avoid negative influences that undermine your confidence.

2. **Embrace Uncertainty:** Uncertainty is a natural part of life. Embrace it with curiosity and openness rather than fear.

- **Stay Flexible:** Be open to new experiences and adaptable to change. Embrace the unknown as an opportunity for growth.

- **Focus on the Present:** Stay present and focus on what you can control. Avoid worrying about the future or dwelling on the past.

- **Practice Gratitude:** Practice gratitude to stay grounded and positive. Reflect on the things you're grateful for and appreciate the present moment.

3. **Develop Resilience:** Resilience is the ability to bounce back from setbacks and challenges.

- **Stay Persistent:** Keep pushing forward, even when things get tough. Stay committed to your goals, and don't give up.

- **Learn from Setbacks:** View setbacks as opportunities for growth. Reflect on what you can learn and how you can improve.

- **Practice Self-Care:** Take care of your physical and mental well-being. Self-care helps you stay strong and resilient.

4. **Cultivate Self-Compassion:** Self-compassion involves treating yourself with kindness and understanding.

- **Be Kind to Yourself:** Avoid harsh self-criticism and treat yourself with the kindness you would offer a friend.

- **Acknowledge Your Efforts:** Recognize and celebrate your efforts toward your goals and challenges. Appreciate your hard work and dedication.

- **Practice Mindfulness:** Practice mindfulness to stay present and non-judgmental. Mindfulness helps you stay connected to yourself with compassion and acceptance.

Activities to Build Confidence

Here are some activities to help you build and radiate confidence:

1. **Confidence Journal:** Keep a confidence journal where you write about your accomplishments, strengths, and positive experiences. Reflect on your growth and progress. Use your journal to track your goals and celebrate your successes.

2. **Power Poses:** Practice power poses to boost your confidence. Power poses are body positions that make you feel more confident and powerful. Here are a few to try:

   - **The Wonder Woman Pose:** Stand with your feet shoulder-width apart, hands on your hips, and chest lifted.

   - **The Victory Pose:** Stand with your feet together, arms

raised above your head in a V shape, and your head tilted slightly upward.

- ○ **The Confidence Pose:** Stand with your feet shoulder-width apart, hands clasped behind your back, and chest open.

Hold each pose for two minutes and notice how it affects your confidence.

1. **Affirmations:** Use positive affirmations to boost your confidence. Write down affirmations like "I am confident," "I believe in myself," and "I can achieve my goals." Repeat them daily to reinforce your self-belief.

2. **Visualization:** Practice visualization to build confidence and overcome fears. Imagine yourself succeeding in challenging situations and achieving your goals. Focus on the positive emotions and outcomes. Visualization can help you stay motivated and confident.

3. **Goal Setting:** Set specific and achievable goals to build confidence. Break larger goals into smaller, manageable steps. Track your progress and celebrate each achievement. Setting and achieving goals helps you feel accomplished and build self-belief.

Radiating confidence and facing your fears are essential for personal growth and success. By confidently standing tall and embracing challenges, you can overcome obstacles and achieve your dreams. Remember, confidence comes from within and can be developed through positive self-talk, goal-setting, and self-care.

Stay curious, stay positive, and remain persistent, Supergirl. You have the strength to radiate confidence and face your fears with courage and resilience. Embrace the journey, celebrate your progress, and keep striving for improvement. The world is full of opportunities for growth and success – go out there and seize them!

CHAPTER NINE

Understanding Money Matters

Budgeting Basics

Hello, Supergirl! Understanding money matters is essential for making informed financial decisions and achieving your goals. Learning to budget and save wisely will set you up for a lifetime of economic stability and independence. This section will explore budgeting basics and smart saving tips to help you manage your money effectively. Let's get started!

Why Budgeting is Important

Budgeting is creating a plan for how you will spend and save your money. It helps you track your income and expenses, prioritize your spending, and ensure you have enough money for your needs and goals. Here are some reasons why budgeting is important:

- **Financial Control:** Budgeting gives you control over your finances, helping you make informed decisions and avoid overspending.

- **Goal Achievement:** A budget helps you allocate money towards your financial goals, such as saving for a trip, buying a new gadget, or building an emergency fund.

- **Debt Management:** Budgeting helps you manage and pay off debts by ensuring you have enough money to make regular payments.

- **Stress Reduction:** Knowing where your money is going and having a plan can reduce financial stress and anxiety.

Steps to Create a Budget

Creating a budget involves several key steps. Let's break down the process to make it easy and manageable:

Determine Your Income: Start by calculating your total monthly income. This can include:

Allowance: Money given to you by your parents or guardians.

Job Earnings: Income from part-time jobs, babysitting, or other work.

Gifts and Bonuses: Money received as gifts or bonuses.

List Your Expenses: Next, list all your monthly expenses. These can be categorized into fixed expenses and variable expenses:

Fixed Expenses: Regular, consistent expenses that stay mostly the same monthly. Examples include:

1. Phone bill

2. Subscription services (e.g., streaming services)

3. Savings contributions

Variable Expenses: Expenses that can vary each month. Examples include:

1. Food and snacks

2. Entertainment (e.g., movies, games)

3. Clothing and accessories

4. Transportation (e.g., bus fare, gas)

Track Your Spending: Track all your spending for a month to see where your money is going. Keep receipts, use a spending app, or write down your purchases in a notebook. This will help you identify patterns and areas where you might be overspending.

1. **Compare Income and Expenses:** Compare your total monthly income to your total monthly expenses. If your

costs exceed your income, you'll need to adjust your spending or find ways to increase your income. If you have leftover money, you can allocate it towards savings or other financial goals.

2. **Set Financial Goals:** Set specific financial goals to guide your budgeting. These can be short-term goals (e.g., saving for a concert ticket) or long-term goals (e.g., building an emergency fund). Write down your goals and prioritize them.

3. **Create a Spending Plan:** Create a spending plan based on your income, expenses, and financial goals. Allocate money for each expense category and set limits to ensure you stay within your budget. Make sure to include savings in your spending plan.

4. **Review and Adjust Your Budget:** Your budget is flexible. Review and adjust it regularly to reflect changes in your income, expenses, and financial goals. Make any necessary adjustments to stay on track.

Budgeting Tools and Apps

Several tools and apps can help you create and manage your budget. Here are a few popular options:

- **Mint:** Mint is a free budgeting app that helps you track your spending, set financial goals, and monitor your progress. It syncs with your bank accounts and categorizes your transactions automatically.

- **YNAB (You Need A Budget):** YNAB is a budgeting app that helps you plan for future expenses and build a financial buffer. It offers a free trial, but there is a subscription fee for continued use.

- **EveryDollar:** EveryDollar is a budgeting app that allows you to create a monthly budget and track your spending. It offers both a free version and a paid version with additional features.

- **Goodbudget:** Goodbudget is an envelope budgeting app that helps you allocate money for different spending categories. It offers both free and paid plans.

Choose a tool or app that works best for you and fits your needs. These tools can make budgeting more accessible and more efficient.

Common Budgeting Mistakes to Avoid

Here are some common budgeting mistakes to watch out for:

- **Underestimating Expenses:** Be realistic about your spending and include all expenses in your budget. Underestimating expenses can lead to overspending and financial stress.

- **Not Tracking Spending:** Track your spending regularly to ensure you stay within your budget. Failing to do so can lead to unintentional overspending.

- **Ignoring Savings:** Make savings a priority in your budget. Ignoring savings can leave you unprepared for emergencies and hinder your financial goals.

- **Being Too Restrictive:** While sticking to your budget is essential, being too restrictive can make it challenging to maintain. Allow for some flexibility and occasional treats.

Smart Saving Tips

Saving money is essential to managing your finances and achieving your financial goals. Whether saving for a specific purchase, building an emergency fund, or planning for the future, intelligent saving habits can help you reach your goals faster. Let's explore some practical saving tips and strategies.

Why Saving is Important

Saving money provides financial security and flexibility. Here are some reasons why saving is essential:

- **Emergency Fund:** An emergency fund helps cover unexpected expenses, such as medical bills, car repairs, or sudden job loss. It provides a financial safety net and reduces stress during emergencies.

- **Achieving Goals:** Saving money allows you to achieve your financial goals, whether buying a new gadget, going on a trip, or investing in your education.

- **Financial Independence:** Saving helps you build financial independence and reduces reliance on credit or loans. It gives you the freedom to make choices without financial constraints.

- **Building Wealth:** Saving and investing money over time can help you build wealth and secure your financial future.

How to Save Money

Here are some practical tips and strategies to help you save money:

Pay Yourself First: One of the most effective saving strategies is to pay yourself first. This means setting aside a portion of your income for savings before you spend on anything else.

1. **Set a Savings Goal:** Determine how much you want to save each month. Start with a small, achievable amount and gradually increase it over time.

2. **Automate Savings:** Set up automatic transfers from your checking account to your savings account. This ensures that a portion of your income goes directly into savings without

the temptation to spend it.

Create a Savings Plan: Having a clear savings plan can help you stay focused and motivated.

1. **Define Your Goals:** Identify your short-term and long-term savings goals. Write them down and set specific, measurable targets.

2. **Set a Timeline:** Determine when you want to achieve each goal. Break down your goals into smaller milestones and set deadlines for each milestone.

3. **Track Your Progress:** Monitor your savings progress regularly. Adjust your plan as needed to stay on track.

Cut Unnecessary Expenses: Reducing unnecessary expenses can free up more money for savings.

1. **Review Subscriptions:** Cancel subscriptions or memberships you no longer use or need.

2. **Limit Dining Out:** Reduce the frequency of eating out or ordering takeout. Cook meals at home to save money.

3. **Shop Smart:** Look for discounts, use coupons, and compare prices before purchasing. Avoid impulse buying and make a shopping list to stick to your budget.

4. **Reduce Utility Bills:** Conserve energy to save on utility

bills. Turn off lights and appliances when not in use, use energy-efficient bulbs, and unplug chargers.

Save on Transportation: Transportation costs can add up quickly.

1. **Carpool:** Share rides with friends or family members to save on gas and reduce wear and tear on your car.

2. **Public Transportation:** Use public transportation, such as buses or trains, to save on fuel and parking costs.

3. **Bike or Walk:** Consider biking or walking for short distances instead of driving. It's not only cost-effective but also good for your health.

Save on Entertainment: Entertainment expenses can be a significant part of your budget.

1. **Free Activities:** Look for free or low-cost activities in your community, such as hiking, visiting parks, or attending local events.

2. **Library Resources:** Borrow books, movies, and music from the library instead of buying them.

3. **Streaming Services:** To reduce costs, consider sharing streaming service subscriptions with family or friends.

Set Up a Separate Savings Account: Having a separate savings account can help you keep your savings organized and prevent you from dipping into your savings for everyday expenses.

1. **Choose an Account:** Look for a high-yield savings account with a competitive interest rate. Compare different banks and credit unions to find the best option.

2. **Automate Transfers:** Set up automatic transfers from your checking account to your savings account. This ensures that you consistently save a portion of your income.

Take Advantage of Discounts and Rewards: Look for opportunities to save money through discounts, rewards, and cashback programs.

1. **Student Discounts:** Take advantage of discounts offered by retailers, restaurants, and entertainment venues. Always carry your student ID and ask if discounts are available.

2. **Cashback Apps:** Use cashback apps and websites to earn money back on purchases. Popular options include Rakuten, Ibotta, and Honey.

3. **Loyalty Programs:** Sign up for loyalty programs at stores you frequently visit. Earn points and rewards for your purchases and redeem them for discounts or free items.

Invest Wisely: Investing your money can help it grow and achieve long-term financial goals.

1. **Savings Accounts:** Although traditional savings accounts offer low-interest rates, high-yield savings accounts and certificates of deposit (CDs) can provide better returns.

2. **Stocks and Bonds:** Investing in stocks and bonds can offer higher returns, but they also come with higher risks. Consider starting with low-cost index funds or exchange-traded funds (ETFs).

3. **Retirement Accounts:** If you have access to a retirement account, such as a 401(k) or IRA, take advantage of it. Contributing to a retirement account can provide tax benefits and help you build wealth for the future.

Setting Financial Goals

Setting financial goals is crucial to managing your money and achieving financial success. Here's how to set practical financial goals:

1. **Define Your Goals:** Identify what you want to achieve with your money. Your goals can be short-term (e.g., saving for a new phone), medium-term (e.g., saving for a car), or long-term (e.g., saving for college or retirement). Write down your goals and be specific.

2. **Prioritize Your Goals:** Determine which goals are most

important to you and prioritize them. Focus on achieving your high-priority goals first while still making progress on others.

3. **Set Realistic Targets:** Set realistic and achievable targets for each goal. Consider your income, expenses, and timeframe. Break down larger goals into smaller, manageable milestones.

4. **Create an Action Plan:** Develop a detailed action plan to achieve your goals. Identify the steps you need to take and the resources you'll need. Set deadlines for each step and track your progress.

5. **Review and Adjust:** Regularly review your goals and progress. Adjust your action plan as needed to stay on track. Celebrate your achievements and stay motivated.

Building Good Financial Habits

Building good financial habits is essential for long-term financial success. Here are some habits to develop:

1. **Track Your Spending:** Track your spending to stay aware of where your money is going. Record your expenses using a budgeting app, spreadsheet, or notebook.

2. **Pay Yourself First:** Make saving a priority by paying yourself first. Set aside a portion of your income for savings

before spending on anything else.

3. **Avoid Impulse Purchases:** Avoid impulse purchases by taking time to think before buying. Ask yourself if the purchase is necessary and if it matches your financial goals.

4. **Live Within Your Means:** Live within your means by spending less than you earn. Avoid taking on unnecessary debt and focus on saving and investing for the future.

5. **Stay Informed:** Stay informed about personal finance and money management. Read books, attend workshops, and follow financial blogs to expand your knowledge.

Resources for Financial Education

Here are some resources to help you learn more about personal finance and money management:

Books: Some recommended books on personal finance include:

- "Rich Dad Poor Dad" by Robert T. Kiyosaki

- "The Total Money Makeover" by Dave Ramsey

- "Your Money or Your Life" by Vicki Robin and Joe Dominguez

- "I Will Teach You to Be Rich" by Ramit Sethi

Online Courses: Many websites offer free or low-cost courses on personal finance. Some popular options include:

- **Khan Academy:** Offers free courses on personal finance and economics.

- **Coursera:** Provides courses from universities and institutions on various financial topics.

- **Udemy:** Offers affordable courses on budgeting, saving, investing, and more.

Financial Blogs and Websites: Some helpful blogs and websites for financial education include:

- **NerdWallet:** Offers tips and advice on budgeting, saving, and investing.

- **The Simple Dollar:** Provides practical advice on personal finance and money management.

- **Investopedia:** Offers in-depth articles and resources on investing and financial planning.

Podcasts: Financial podcasts can provide valuable insights and tips. Some recommended podcasts include:

- **"The Dave Ramsey Show":** Offers practical advice on budgeting, saving, and debt management.

- **"So Money" with Farnoosh Torabi:** Features interviews

with financial experts and successful individuals.

- **"Afford Anything" with Paula Pant:** Focuses on financial independence and intelligent money management.

Understanding money matters and developing good habits are essential for financial stability and success. By learning budgeting basics and smart saving tips, you can take control of your finances, achieve your goals, and build a secure financial future.

Remember, financial literacy is a lifelong journey. Stay curious, stay informed, and continue to develop your money management skills. With the knowledge and strategies you've learned in this chapter, you have the strength to make wise financial decisions and create a bright future, Supergirl!

CHAPTER TEN

Household Tasks

Everyday Chores

Hey, Supergirl! Mastering household tasks is essential to growing up and becoming more independent. Learning to manage everyday chores helps keep your living space clean and organized and builds valuable life skills like responsibility, time management, and self-sufficiency. This section will explore everyday chores and tips for tidying your space. Let's get started!

Why Mastering Household Tasks is Important

Understanding how to perform household tasks efficiently offers numerous benefits:

- **Independence:** Managing household tasks independently makes you more self-reliant and confident.

- **Responsibility:** Regularly completing chores teaches you responsibility and accountability.

- **Time Management:** Managing chores and other activities helps improve your time management skills.

- **Cleanliness:** Keeping your space tidy promotes a healthier and more pleasant living environment.

- **Skill Building:** Learning household tasks equips you with essential skills you'll need.

Getting Started with Everyday Chores

Daily chores must be done regularly to maintain a clean and functional living space. Here are some typical everyday chores and how to tackle them:

Making Your Bed: Making your bed each morning sets a positive tone for the day and makes your room look neat.

1. **Straighten the Sheets:** Pull the sheets tight and smooth out any wrinkles.

2. **Arrange Pillows:** Fluff and arrange your pillows neatly at the head of the bed.

3. **Add a Comforter or Blanket:** Spread your comforter or blanket evenly over the bed.

4. **Finishing Touches:** Add any decorative pillows or throws for a polished look.

Dishes: Keeping up with the dishes prevents a buildup of dirty dishes and keeps your kitchen tidy.

1. **Before Cooking:** Start with an empty sink and dishwasher (if you have one).

2. **As You Cook:** Wash utensils, bowls, and pans as you go to avoid a big pile at the end.

3. **After Meals:** Rinse dishes and load them into the dishwasher or wash them by hand immediately after eating.

4. **Dry and Put Away:** Dry dishes with a clean towel and put them away in their designated spots.

Laundry: Doing laundry regularly ensures you have clean clothes and linens.

1. **Sort Clothes:** Separate clothes by color (whites, darks, colors) and fabric type (delicates, heavy fabrics).

2. **Check Labels:** Follow care labels on clothing for washing instructions.

3. **Load the Washer:** Add the appropriate amount of detergent and load the washer. Avoid overloading it.

4. **Dry Clothes:** Transfer clothes to the dryer or hang them to dry, depending on the fabric.

5. **Fold and Put Away:** Fold clothes neatly and put them away in drawers or closets.

Sweeping and Vacuuming: Regular sweeping and vacuuming keep your floors clean and free of dust and debris.

1. **Sweep Floors:** Use a broom and dustpan to sweep hard floors, focusing on corners and under furniture.

2. **Vacuum Carpets:** Use a vacuum cleaner to clean carpets and rugs. Move furniture as needed to reach all areas.

3. **Spot Clean:** Address any spills or stains immediately to prevent them from setting in.

Dusting: Dusting helps remove allergens and keeps surfaces clean.

1. **Use a Microfiber Cloth:** A microfiber cloth traps dust better than a regular cloth.

2. **Start High:** Begin dusting from the top (e.g., shelves, ceiling fans) and work your way down.

3. **Remember Corners:** Dust corners, baseboards, and behind furniture.

4. **Polish Surfaces:** Use furniture polish for wooden surfaces

to add shine and protection.

Cleaning the Bathroom: Keeping the bathroom clean is essential for hygiene.

1. **Wipe Down Surfaces:** Use a disinfectant wipe or spray to clean countertops, sinks, and faucets.

2. **Clean the Toilet:** Use toilet cleaner and a brush to scrub the inside of the toilet. Wipe the outside with a disinfectant.

3. **Shower/Tub:** Clean the shower or tub with a bathroom cleaner. Scrub tiles and grout as needed.

4. **Mirrors and Glass:** Clean mirrors and glass surfaces with a glass cleaner for a streak-free shine.

5. **Replace Towels:** Replace used towels with clean ones and wash the used towels regularly.

Taking Out the Trash: Taking out the trash regularly prevents unpleasant odors and keeps your space clean.

1. **Empty Trash Cans:** Regularly empty trash cans in your room, bathroom, and kitchen.

2. **Recycle:** Separate recyclable materials (paper, plastic, glass) and place them in the recycling bin.

3. **Compost:** Add food scraps and other compostable

materials if you have a compost bin.

4. **Replace Liners:** Replace trash can liners with new ones to keep cans clean.

Creating a Chore Schedule

A chore schedule helps you stay organized and complete all household tasks regularly. Here's how to create an effective chore schedule:

1. **List All Chores:** List all the household chores that need to be done regularly. Include daily, weekly, and monthly tasks.

2. **Assign Chores:** Assign chores to specific days of the week. For example:

   ◦ **Daily:** Make the bed, wash dishes, wipe down surfaces.

   ◦ **Weekly:** Laundry, vacuuming, dusting, bathroom cleaning.

   ◦ **Monthly:** Deep cleaning, organizing closets, cleaning windows.

3. **Set Time Limits:** Allocate a specific amount of time for each chore. This helps you manage your time effectively and prevents chores from becoming overwhelming.

4. **Use a Chore Chart:** Create a chore chart to track your

progress. You can use a physical chart or a digital app. Mark off completed chores to stay motivated and accountable.

Tips for Staying Motivated

Keeping up with household chores can sometimes feel like a drag. Here are some tips to stay motivated and make chores more enjoyable:

1. **Set Goals and Rewards:** Set specific goals for completing chores and reward yourself for achieving them. For example, after completing all your weekly tasks, treat yourself to a movie night or a special snack.

2. **Make It Fun:** Turn chores into fun by listening to music or podcasts while you work. You can also turn it into a game by timing yourself and trying to beat your previous record.

3. **Work with Others:** If you live with family or roommates, divide the chores and work together. Working as a team makes chores more enjoyable and gets them done faster.

4. **Stay Consistent:** Consistency is critical to maintaining a clean and organized space. Stick to your chore schedule and make it a habit. Over time, it will become a natural part of your routine.

Keeping Your Space Tidy

In addition to completing everyday chores, keeping your space tidy is essential for maintaining a clean and organized environment. Here are some tips and strategies for keeping your space tidy:

Decluttering Your Space: Decluttering helps create a more organized and stress-free environment.

1. **Start Small:** To avoid feeling overwhelmed, begin with a small area, such as a drawer or a shelf, and gradually work through larger areas.

2. **Sort Items:** Sort items into three categories: Keep, donate, and discard. Keep items that you use regularly and have sentimental value. Donate items that are in good condition but no longer needed. Discard items that are broken or unusable.

3. **Organize and Store:** Organize the items you're keeping in a logical and accessible way. Use storage bins, baskets, and shelves to keep things tidy. Label containers to make it easy to find what you need.

4. **Maintain Regularly:** Regularly declutter and reorganize your space to prevent buildup. Set aside time each month to review your belongings and make necessary adjustments.

Organizing Your Space: Organizing your space helps you stay efficient and reduces clutter.

1. **Bedroom:** Use hangers, shelves, and bins to organize

clothes, shoes, and accessories. Arrange items by category (e.g., shirts, pants, dresses) and color. Use drawer dividers to separate socks, underwear, and accessories.

2. **Desk:** Keep your desk surface clear by only having essential items like a computer, a notepad, and writing tools. Use desk organizers to store pens, paper, and other supplies. Arrange books and binders by category on shelves.

3. **Bathroom:** Store toiletries in cabinets or drawers to keep countertops clear. Use trays or small baskets to organize frequently used items. Maximize cabinet space with shelf organizers.

4. **Kitchen:** Use clear containers to store dry goods like pasta, rice, and cereal. Label containers and arrange items by category for easy access. Use drawer dividers to organize utensils and kitchen tools. Store pots and pans in lower cabinets for easy access.

Cleaning Tips for Different Areas

Keeping different areas of your home clean requires specific techniques and tools. Here are some cleaning tips for various regions:

Kitchen:

1. **Counters and Surfaces:** Wipe down counters and surfaces with a disinfectant cleaner after each use.

2. **Sink:** Clean the sink daily to prevent buildup. Use a scrub brush and dish soap to remove residue and stains.

3. **Appliances:** Clean appliances like the microwave, stove, and refrigerator regularly. Wipe down the exterior and clean the interior as needed.

Living Room:

1. **Furniture:** Vacuum and dust furniture regularly. For upholstered furniture, use a fabric cleaner and a wood polish.

2. **Floors:** Sweep or vacuum floors weekly. Use a mop to clean hard floors and a carpet cleaner for rugs and carpets.

3. **Windows:** Clean windows and window sills with a glass cleaner. Wipe down blinds or curtains to remove dust.

Bedroom:

1. **Bedding:** Wash sheets, pillowcases, and blankets weekly. Fluff and rotate pillows regularly to maintain their shape.

2. **Floors:** Sweep or vacuum floors weekly. Use a mop for hard floors and a carpet cleaner for rugs and carpets.

3. **Surfaces:** Dust surfaces like dressers, nightstands, and shelves regularly. Use furniture polish for wooden surfaces.

Bathroom:

1. **Toilet:** Clean the toilet with a toilet cleaner and brush. Wipe down the exterior with a disinfectant.

2. **Sink and Countertops:** Wipe the sink and countertops with a disinfectant cleaner. Pay attention to faucets and handles.

3. **Shower and Tub:** Clean the shower and tub with a bathroom cleaner. Scrub tiles and grout to remove soap scum and mildew.

Maintaining a Tidy Space

Maintaining a tidy space requires consistent effort and good habits. Here are some tips to help you keep your space tidy:

- **Clean as You Go:** Cleaning as you go prevents messes from accumulating. For example, wash dishes immediately after eating, put away clothes after wearing them, and wipe down surfaces after use.

- **Designate Spaces:** Assign a designated space for each item in your home. This will make it easier to find things and prevent clutter. Make it a habit to return items to their designated spaces after use.

- **Regularly Declutter:** Declutter your space regularly to prevent buildup. Set aside time each month to go through your belongings and remove items you no longer need.

- **Set a Cleaning Schedule:** Create a cleaning schedule to ensure all home areas are cleaned regularly. Divide tasks into daily, weekly, and monthly chores and stick to the schedule.

- **Stay Organized:** Use storage solutions like bins, baskets, and shelves to organize your space. Label containers and arrange items logically to make it easy to find what you need.

Tips for Living with Others

Living with family or roommates requires cooperation and communication to maintain a clean and tidy space. Here are some tips for living harmoniously with others:

- **Divide Chores:** Divide household chores among all household members. Create a chore chart to keep track of responsibilities and ensure that everyone contributes.

- **Communicate:** Communicate openly and respectfully about cleaning expectations and preferences. Address any issues or concerns promptly to prevent conflicts.

- **Respect Shared Spaces:** Respect shared spaces by keeping them clean and tidy. Clean up after yourself and be considerate of others' needs and preferences.

- **Support Each Other:** Support each other in maintaining a clean and tidy space. Offer help and encourage each other to stick to the cleaning schedule.

Mastering household tasks and tidying your space are essential skills that contribute to a clean, organized, and pleasant living environment. By learning to manage everyday chores and maintain a tidy space, you can build valuable life skills like responsibility, time management, and self-sufficiency.

Remember, consistency is critical. Stick to your chore schedule, stay organized, and make cleaning and tidying a routine. With these skills and habits, you can create a clean and comfortable home that you can be proud of, Supergirl!

CHAPTER ELEVEN

More Valuable Life Skills

Time Management

Hello, Supergirl! Time management is one of the most valuable life skills you can develop. It helps you make the most of your day, achieve your goals, and maintain a healthy balance between work and play. Effective time management allows you to be more productive, reduce stress, and feel more in control of your life. This section will explore strategies for managing your time effectively and delve into problem-solving strategies to help you navigate challenges and make informed decisions. Let's explore in!

Why Time Management Matters

Good time management skills are essential for several reasons:

1. **Increased Productivity**: Managing your time effectively helps you accomplish more tasks in less time.

2. **Reduced Stress**: Having a clear plan and staying organized minimizes the stress of last-minute rushes and missed deadlines.

3. **Better Work-Life Balance**: Effective time management allows you to balance school, work, hobbies, and relaxation.

4. **Goal Achievement**: Planning your time helps you set and achieve short-term and long-term goals.

Steps to Effective Time Management

Set Clear Goals

Setting clear, specific goals gives you direction and motivation. Here's how to set practical goals:

- **SMART Goals**: Make sure your goals are Specific, Measurable, Achievable, Relevant, and Time-bound. For example, instead of saying, "I want to get better grades," set a goal like "I will study for one hour every day to improve my math grade by the end of the semester."

- **Break Down Goals**: Break larger goals into smaller, manageable tasks. This makes them less overwhelming and more accessible to accomplish.

Prioritize Tasks

Prioritizing tasks helps you focus on what's most important. Here's how to prioritize effectively:

- **Make a To-Do List**: Write down all the tasks you must complete. Include both urgent and non-urgent tasks.

- **Use the Eisenhower Matrix**: Divide your tasks into four categories:

  - **Urgent and Important**: Tasks that need immediate attention (e.g., assignments due tomorrow).

  - **Necessary but Not Urgent**: Tasks that are important but can be scheduled (e.g., studying for a test next week).

  - **Urgent but Not Important**: Tasks that require immediate attention but are not crucial (e.g., responding to non-critical emails).

  - **Not Urgent and Not Important**: Tasks that are neither urgent nor important (e.g., watching TV).

Complete tasks in the "Urgent and Important" category first, then move on to the "Important but Not Urgent" category.

Create a Schedule

Creating a schedule helps you allocate time for each task and stay organized. Here's how to create an effective schedule:

- **Use a Planner or Calendar**: Choose a planner or digital calendar that works for you. Write down your tasks, appointments, and deadlines.

- **Block Time**: Allocate specific blocks of time for each task. Be realistic about how long each task will take.

- **Include Breaks**: Schedule regular breaks to rest and recharge. Avoid overloading your schedule to prevent burnout.

- **Review and Adjust**: Review your schedule regularly and make adjustments as needed. Be flexible and adaptable to changes.

Avoid Procrastination

Procrastination is a common challenge in time management. Here are some tips to overcome procrastination:

- **Set Deadlines**: Set specific deadlines for each task to create a sense of urgency.

- **Use the Pomodoro Technique**: Work for 25 minutes, then take a 5-minute break. Repeat this cycle four times, then take a more extended break.

- **Break Tasks into Smaller Steps**: Breaking tasks into smaller, manageable steps makes them less scary and easier to start.

- **Eliminate Distractions**: To stay focused, identify and eliminate distractions, such as social media or noisy environments.

Stay Organized

Staying organized helps you manage your time more effectively. Here's how to stay organized:

- **Declutter Your Workspace**: Keep your workspace clean and organized to minimize distractions.

- **Use Organizational Tools**: Use to-do lists, planners, and apps to stay organized and track your tasks.

- **Set Up a Filing System**: Organize your documents and materials with a filing system. Use folders, labels, and binders to keep everything in order.

Delegate Tasks

Delegating tasks can help you manage your workload and focus on what's most important. Here's how to delegate effectively:

- **Identify Tasks to Delegate**: Determine which tasks, such as chores or group project responsibilities, can be delegated to others.

- **Choose the Right Person**: Delegate tasks to someone with the skills and availability to complete them.

- **Provide Clear Instructions**: Communicate the task, expectations, and deadlines to the person you're delegating.

- **Follow-up**: Check in on the progress of delegated tasks to ensure they are being completed as expected.

Tools and Apps for Time Management

Several tools and apps can help you manage your time effectively. Here are a few popular options:

- **Google Calendar**: A free digital calendar that allows you to schedule events, set reminders, and share your calendar with others.

- **Trello**: A project management app that uses boards, lists, and cards to organize tasks and track progress.

- **Todoist**: A to-do list app that helps you create and manage tasks, set deadlines, and prioritize tasks.

- **Notion**: An all-in-one workspace that combines notes, tasks, databases, and calendars for comprehensive time management.

- **Forest**: A focused app that helps you stay off your phone and concentrate on tasks by growing virtual trees.

Common Time Management Pitfalls to Avoid

Here are some common time management pitfalls to watch out for:

- **Overcommitting**: Avoid taking on too many tasks at once. Be realistic about your accomplishments and learn to say no when necessary.

- **Multitasking**: Multitasking can reduce your productivity and increase errors. Focus on one task at a time to work more efficiently.

- **Ignoring Breaks**: Skipping breaks can lead to burnout and reduced productivity. Schedule regular breaks to rest and recharge.

- **Perfectionism**: Striving for perfection can lead to procrastination and delays. Aim for progress, not perfection.

Problem-Solving Strategies

Practical problem-solving skills are essential for finding your way to challenges and making informed decisions. You can confidently approach obstacles and find creative solutions by developing strong problem-solving abilities. Let's explore some strategies for effective problem-solving.

Why Problem-Solving Skills Matter

Problem-solving skills are important for several reasons:

Critical Thinking: Problem-solving requires critical thinking and analysis, helping you make informed decisions.

Adaptability: Effective problem-solving helps you adapt to changes and unexpected challenges.

Confidence: Successfully solving problems boosts your confidence and self-efficacy.

Innovation: Problem-solving encourages creativity and innovation, leading to new ideas and solutions.

Steps to Effective Problem-Solving

Identify the Problem

The first step in solving a problem is identifying and defining it clearly. Here's how to identify the problem effectively:

- **Describe the Problem**: Write down a clear and concise description of the problem. Include relevant details and context.

- **Ask Questions**: Ask questions to understand the problem better. Consider what, why, when, where, and how.

- Gather Information: Collect relevant information and data to understand the problem better.

Analyze the Problem

Analyzing the problem helps you understand its root cause and identify potential solutions. Here's how to diagnose the problem:

- **Break Down the Problem**: Divide the problem into smaller components or parts. This makes it easier to analyze and understand.

- **Identify Causes**: Determine the underlying causes of the problem. Consider factors that may be contributing to the issue.

- **Evaluate Impact**: Assess the impact of the problem on different areas or individuals. Consider both short-term and long-term effects.

Generate Possible Solutions

Generating multiple solutions helps you explore different approaches to solving the problem. Here's how to create possible solutions:

- **Brainstorm Ideas**: Write down all possible solutions, even if they seem unconventional. Initially, aim for quantity over quality.

- **Encourage Creativity**: Think creatively and explore innovative solutions. Consider different perspectives and approaches.

- **Involve Others**: Collaborate with others to generate ideas.

Different viewpoints can lead to new and effective solutions.

Evaluate and Select Solutions

Evaluating and selecting the best solution makes sure that you choose an effective and feasible approach. Here's how to evaluate and select solutions:

- **List Pros and Cons**: Create a list of pros and cons for each solution. Consider factors such as effectiveness, feasibility, and potential impact.

- **Assess Resources**: Evaluate the resources required for each solution, including time, money, and effort.

- **Choose the Best Solution**: Select the solution that offers the most benefits and is most feasible to implement.

Implement the Solution

Implementing the chosen solution involves putting the plan into action. Here's how to implement the solution effectively:

- **Create an Action Plan**: Develop a detailed action plan that outlines the steps required to implement the solution. Assign responsibilities and set deadlines.

- Communicate: Communicate the plan to all relevant individuals and stakeholders. Make sure everyone understands their roles and responsibilities.

- **Monitor Progress**: Regularly monitor the progress of the implementation. Track milestones and make adjustments as needed.

Evaluate the Results

Evaluating the results helps you determine whether the solution was effective and identify any areas for improvement. Here's how to evaluate the results:

- **Measure Outcomes**: Measure the outcomes and results of the implemented solution. Compare them to the expected results and goals.

- **Gather Feedback**: Collect feedback from relevant individuals and stakeholders. Consider their perspectives and experiences.

- **Identify Lessons Learned**: Reflect on the problem-solving process and identify lessons learned. Consider what worked well and what could be improved.

Problem-Solving Techniques

Here are some problem-solving techniques that can help you approach challenges effectively:

Mind Mapping

Mind mapping is a visual technique that helps you organize information and ideas. Here's how to create a mind map:

- **Start with the Problem**: Write the problem in the center of a blank page.

- **Add Branches**: Create branches for different aspects of the problem, such as causes, effects, and potential solutions.

- **Expand Further**: Add sub-branches to each main branch to explore details and connections.

SWOT Analysis

SWOT analysis is a technique that helps you evaluate strengths, weaknesses, opportunities, and threats. Here's how to conduct a SWOT analysis:

- **Identify Strengths**: List the strengths of the situation or solution. Consider internal factors that provide an advantage.

- **Identify Weaknesses**: List the weaknesses of the situation or solution. Consider internal factors that present challenges.

- **Identify Opportunities**: List the opportunities available. Consider external factors that can be leveraged.

- **Identify Threats**: List the threats that may impact the situation or solution. Consider external factors that pose risks.

Root Cause Analysis

Root cause analysis helps you identify the underlying cause of a problem. Here's how to conduct a root cause analysis:

- **Define the Problem**: Clearly define the problem and its impact.

- **Ask, "Why?"**: Ask "Why?" multiple times to investigate the cause of the problem. Each answer should lead to another "Why?" question.

- **Identify the Root Cause**: Continue asking "Why?" until you identify the root cause of the problem.

Brainstorming

Brainstorming is a technique that encourages creative thinking and idea generation. Here's how to conduct a brainstorming session:

- **Set a Goal**: Define the brainstorming session's goal, such as generating solutions for a specific problem.

- **Encourage Free Thinking**: Encourage participants to share any ideas that come to mind. Avoid judgment or criticism during the session.

- **Record Ideas**: Write down all ideas on a whiteboard or notepad. Consider using sticky notes for easy organization.

- **Evaluate Ideas**: After the session, evaluate the ideas and select the most promising ones for further consideration.

Common Problem-Solving Challenges and How to Overcome Them

Here are some common challenges you may encounter during problem-solving and how to overcome them:

Lack of Information

Sometimes, you may need more information to make informed decisions. Here's how to overcome this challenge:

- **Research**: Research to gather relevant information and data. Use reliable sources such as books, articles, and reputable websites.

- **Ask Questions**: Seek information from knowledgeable individuals or experts. Ask specific questions to gain insights and clarity.

- **Analyze Data**: Organize and analyze the data you've collected. Look for patterns and trends that can inform your decision-making.

Groupthink

Groupthink occurs when a group prioritizes consensus over critical thinking and explorers' viewpoints. Here's how to overcome groupthink:

- Encourage Diverse Opinions: Create an environment where explorers' opinions are welcomed and valued. Encourage participants to share different perspectives.

- Assign a Devil's Advocate: Designate someone to challenge ideas and assumptions. This will help ensure that all options are thoroughly evaluated.

- Use Anonymous Feedback: Collect anonymous feedback from participants to reduce the pressure to conform. This encourages honest and explorers input.

Emotional Influence

Emotions can impact your ability to think clearly and make rational decisions. Here's how to manage emotions during problem-solving:

- **Stay Calm**: Take deep breaths and stay calm when faced with a problem. Avoid making decisions when you're feeling highly emotional.

- Reflect on Emotions: Consider how your emotions might be influencing your thinking. Separate your emotions from the problem at hand.

- Seek Support: Talk to a trusted friend or mentor for support and perspective. This can help you stay objective and focused.

Overwhelm

Feeling overwhelmed by the complexity of a problem can hinder your ability to find solutions. Here's how to overcome overwhelm:

- **Break Down the Problem**: Divide the problem into smaller, manageable parts. Focus on one part at a time to reduce overwhelm.

- **Prioritize Tasks**: Prioritize tasks based on their importance and urgency. Address the most critical tasks first.

- **Take Breaks**: Take regular breaks to rest and recharge. Avoid working on the problem for extended periods without breaks.

Developing a Problem-Solving Mindset

Developing a problem-solving mindset involves adopting attitudes and behaviors that support effective problem-solving. Here's how to cultivate a problem-solving mindset:

Stay Curious

Cultivate a sense of curiosity and a desire to learn. Approach problems with an open mind and a willingness to explore new ideas and solutions.

Embrace Challenges

View challenges as opportunities for growth and learning. Embrace challenges with a positive attitude and a determination to find solutions.

Be Persistent

When faced with obstacles, stay persistent and determined. Keep trying different approaches, and keep going until you find a solution.

Learn from Mistakes

View mistakes as valuable learning experiences. Reflect on what went wrong and how you can improve in the future.

Collaborate

Work collaboratively with others to find solutions. Value explorer's perspectives and leverage the strengths of your team.

Mastering time management and problem-solving skills are essential for achieving your goals and effectively finding your way. You can improve productivity, reduce stress, and make informed decisions by managing your time wisely, setting clear goals, and developing strong problem-solving strategies.

Remember, these skills take time and practice to develop. Stay patient, stay persistent, and keep learning. With the knowledge and strategies you've learned in this chapter, you can manage your time effectively and solve problems confidently, Supergirl!

CHAPTER TWELVE

Embracing Technology

Safe Internet Practices

Hello, Supergirl! In today's world, technology is an integral part of our lives. It connects, entertains, and provides endless opportunities for learning and growth. But it's essential to use technology wisely and safely. Understanding safe Internet practices and utilizing educational tools can help you make the most of the digital world. In this section, we'll explore strategies for staying safe online and maximizing the benefits of educational technology. Let's get started!

Why Safe Internet Practices Matter

The internet is a strong tool, but it also comes with risks. Safe internet habits are crucial for protecting your personal information, avoiding harmful content, and maintaining your well-being. Here are some reasons why safe internet practices matter:

Protecting Personal Information: Safeguarding personal information helps prevent identity theft and privacy breaches.

Avoiding Scams and Malware: Safe internet practices help you avoid scams, phishing attempts, and malicious software.

Maintaining Digital Well-Being: Managing your online presence and screen time contributes to your overall well-being and mental health.

Ensuring Positive Online Interactions: Practicing safe and respectful online behavior fosters positive interactions and relationships.

Steps to Make Sure Safe Internet Practices

Protect Your Personal Information

Your personal information is valuable and should be protected. Here's how to keep your personal information safe online:

- **Use Strong Passwords**: Create strong, unique passwords for your online accounts. Use uppercase and lowercase letters, numbers, and special characters. Avoid using easily guessable information like your name or birthdate.

- **Enable Two-Factor Authentication**: For an extra layer

of security, enable two-factor authentication (2FA). This requires you to verify your identity using a second method, such as a text message or authentication app, in addition to your password.

- **Be Cautious with Personal Details**: Avoid sharing sensitive personal information, such as your full name, address, phone number, and financial details, on public websites or social media platforms.

- **Review Privacy Settings**: Regularly review and update the privacy settings on your social media accounts and other online platforms to control who can see your information.

Recognize and Avoid Scams

Scams and phishing attempts are common online. Here's how to recognize and avoid them:

- **Be Skeptical of Unsolicited Messages**: Be cautious of unsolicited messages, emails, or pop-ups asking for personal information or money. Scammers often pose as legitimate organizations or individuals.

- **Verify Sources**: Before clicking on links or providing information, verify the legitimacy of websites and email addresses. Look for signs like secure URLs (starting with "https://") and official contact details.

- **Avoid Clicking on Suspicious Links**: Avoid clicking on links or downloading attachments from unknown or suspicious sources. These could contain malware or lead to phishing sites.

- **Report Suspicious Activity**: Report suspicious emails, messages, or websites to the appropriate authorities or platforms. This helps protect others from falling victim to scams.

Practice Safe Browsing

Safe browsing habits help protect you from harmful content and malware. Here's how to practice safe browsing:

- **Use Trusted Websites**: For information, shopping, and downloads, stick to trusted and reputable websites. Look for secure connections (https://) and recognizable domain names.

- Install Security Software: Use antivirus and anti-malware software to protect your device from malicious software. Keep the software updated to ensure the latest protection.

- **Avoid Illegal Downloads**: Avoid downloading pirated software, music, or movies. These often come with hidden malware and can lead to legal consequences.

- **Be Cautious with Public Wi-Fi**: Public Wi-Fi networks

can be less secure. Avoid accessing sensitive information, such as online banking, on public Wi-Fi. Use a virtual private network (VPN) for added security.

Manage Your Digital Footprint

Your digital footprint is the trail of information you leave behind online. Here's how to manage your digital footprint:

- **Think Before You Post**: Consider the potential impact of your posts before sharing them. Avoid sharing sensitive or personal information publicly.

- **Review Old Posts**: Regularly review and delete old posts, comments, and photos that no longer reflect who you are or that you no longer wish to share.

- Use Anonymity Wisely: Although anonymity can offer privacy, it can also lead to irresponsible behavior. Use it wisely and avoid posting harmful or inappropriate content.

- **Be Mindful of Sharing**: Be cautious when sharing content created by others. Respect copyright and privacy laws, and always give credit where it's due.

Respect Others Online

Respectful online behavior contributes to a positive digital environment. Here's how to respect others online:

- **Be Kind and Considerate**: Treat others with kindness and respect in all online interactions. Avoid engaging in cyberbullying, harassment, or harmful behavior.

- **Practice Digital Etiquette**: Follow digital etiquette (netiquette) by being polite, using appropriate language, and respecting others' opinions and boundaries.

- **Report Inappropriate Behavior**: Report cyberbullying, harassment, or inappropriate content to the relevant platform or authority. Support others who may be experiencing online abuse.

- **Think Before You Comment**: Think carefully before commenting on posts or engaging in online discussions. Consider how your words affect others and strive for constructive and positive interactions.

Balancing Screen Time

Managing screen time is essential for maintaining a healthy balance between online and offline activities. Here's how to balance your screen time:

Set Screen Time Limits

Set limits on the amount of time you spend on screens each day. Use built-in screen time settings on your devices or apps like Screen Time (iOS) or Digital Wellbeing (Android) to monitor and control your usage.

Create a Daily Schedule

Create a daily schedule with designated times for online activities, schoolwork, hobbies, physical activity, and relaxation. Please stick to the schedule to ensure a balanced day.

Take Regular Breaks

Take regular breaks from screens to rest your eyes and reduce fatigue. Follow the 20-20-20 rule: every 20 minutes, look at something 20 feet away for at least 20 seconds.

Engage in Offline Activities

Make time for offline activities like reading, drawing, playing sports, or spending time with friends and family. These activities help reduce screen time and promote overall well-being.

Avoid Screen Time Before Bed

Avoid using screens at least an hour before bedtime. Screens emit blue light, which can interfere with sleep. Instead, enjoy relaxing activities like reading a book or practicing mindfulness.

Utilizing Educational Tools

Technology offers many educational tools to improve your learning experience and help you achieve your academic goals. From online resources to educational apps, here's how to make the most of educational technology.

Benefits of Educational Technology

Educational technology provides several benefits:

Access to Information: Technology gives you access to vast information and resources, making learning more comprehensive and convenient.

Interactive Learning: Educational tools often include interactive features that make learning more engaging and effective.

Personalized Learning: Technology allows for personalized learning experiences, adapting to your pace and learning style.

Collaboration: Online platforms facilitate peer collaboration, enabling group projects and discussions.

Utilizing Online Resources

Online resources offer various educational content, from videos and articles to interactive exercises. Here's how to make the most of online resources:

Educational Websites

Many reputable educational websites provide high-quality content on various subjects. Here are some popular options:

- **Khan Academy**: Offers free video lessons and exercises on a wide range of subjects, including math, science, history, and more.

- **Coursera**: Provides online courses on various topics from universities and institutions. Some courses are free, while others require payment.

- **edX** offers online courses from top universities and organizations. Many courses are free to audit, and paid certificates are available.

- **TED-Ed**: Features educational videos and lessons on a variety of topics created by educators and animators.

YouTube Channels

YouTube has many educational channels that offer engaging and informative content. Here are some recommended channels:

- **CrashCourse**: Provides entertaining and educational history, science, and literature videos.

- **SciShow**: Offers videos on scientific topics, from biology and chemistry to physics and astronomy.

- **Minute Physics**: Explains complex physics concepts in short, easy-to-understand videos.

- **AsapSCIENCE**: Covers a wide range of scientific topics in a fun and accessible way.

Online Libraries and Databases

Online libraries and databases provide access to a wealth of books, articles, and academic papers. Here are some useful resources:

- **Project Gutenberg**: Offers over 60,000 free eBooks, including classic literature and non-fiction works.

- **Google Scholar**: Provides access to academic papers, theses, books, and conference papers.

- **JSTOR**: A digital library of academic journals, books, and primary sources. Access may require a subscription or institutional affiliation.

Educational Apps and Tools

Educational apps and tools can improve your learning experience and help you stay organized. Here are some recommended apps and tools:

Note-Taking Apps

Note-taking apps help you organize your notes and keep track of important information. Here are some popular options:

- **Evernote** allows you to create and organize notes, attach files, and set reminders. It also syncs across all your devices.

- **OneNote**: A digital notebook that lets you take notes, draw, and collaborate with others—Integrates with Microsoft Office.

- **Notion**: An all-in-one workspace for notes, tasks, and projects. Offers a flexible and customizable interface.

Flashcard Apps

Flashcard apps help you study and memorize information effectively. Here are some popular options:

- **Quizlet**: You can create and study flashcards, play learning games, and take practice tests. Offers pre-made flashcards on various subjects.

- Anki: A strengthful flashcard app that uses spaced repetition to help you retain information. Supports images, audio, and video.

- **Brainscape**: Offers flashcards and quizzes on a wide range of subjects. It uses a smart algorithm to optimize your study sessions.

Math and Science Apps

Math and science apps provide interactive lessons and exercises to help you understand complex concepts. Here are some recommended apps:

- **Photomath**: This program lets you take a picture of a

math problem and provides step-by-step solutions. It covers arithmetic, algebra, calculus, and more.

- **Khan Academy**: Offers a comprehensive app with video lessons and exercises on various subjects, including math and science.

- **Wolfram Alpha**: A computational knowledge engine that answers factual questions and solves mathematical problems.

Language Learning Apps

Language learning apps help you learn and practice new languages. Here are some popular options:

- **Duolingo**: Offers gamified language lessons in a wide range of languages. Tracks your progress and provides daily practice.

- **Babbel**: Provides interactive language courses designed by experts. Focuses on real-life conversations and practical vocabulary.

- **Rosetta Stone**: Uses immersive lessons to teach new languages. Emphasizes speaking and listening skills.

Remember, when used wisely, technology is a strengthful tool that can open up endless opportunities for growth and learning. Stay curious, stay safe, and make the most of the resources available to you, Supergirl!

CHAPTER THIRTEEN

Developing Healthy Habits

Nutrition and Exercise

Hello, Supergirl! Developing healthy habits is essential for maintaining your physical and mental well-being. Good nutrition, regular exercise, and mindfulness practices can help you feel your best, stay energized, and manage stress effectively. In this section, we'll explore the importance of nutrition, exercise, mindfulness, and relaxation techniques. Let's get started!

Why Nutrition and Exercise Matter

Nutrition and exercise are fundamental components of a healthy lifestyle. This contributes to overall health, boosts energy levels, and helps prevent chronic diseases. Here's why nutrition and exercise matter:

Energy Levels: Proper nutrition and regular exercise help maintain steady energy levels throughout the day.

Physical Health: A balanced diet and physical activity support healthy growth, development, and the functioning of your body.

Mental Health: Nutrition and exercise have a significant impact on your mental health, improving mood, reducing anxiety, and enhancing cognitive function.

Disease Prevention: Healthy eating and regular exercise reduce the risk of chronic diseases such as obesity, diabetes, heart disease, and certain cancers.

Understanding Nutrition

Good nutrition involves consuming various foods that provide the nutrients your body needs to function correctly. Here's a detailed look at the essential components of a healthy diet:

Macronutrients

Macronutrients are nutrients that your body needs in large amounts. They provide energy and are essential for growth and maintenance. The three main macronutrients are:

- Carbohydrates: Carbohydrates are your body's primary source of energy. They are found in grains, fruits, vegetables, and legumes. Choose complex carbohydrates, such as whole grains, that provide sustained energy and are fiber-rich.

- Examples: Whole wheat bread, brown rice, oats, quinoa, sweet potatoes.

- Proteins: Proteins are essential for building and repairing tissues, making enzymes and hormones, and supporting immune function. They are found in animal products and plant-based sources.

  - Examples: Chicken, fish, eggs, beans, lentils, tofu, nuts, and seeds.

- **Fats**: Fats provide energy, support cell growth, protect organs, and help absorb vitamins. Focus on healthy fats, such as unsaturated fats, and limit saturated and trans fats.

  - Examples: Avocados, olive oil, nuts, seeds, fatty fish (like salmon), and flaxseeds.

Micronutrients

Micronutrients are vitamins and minerals that your body needs in smaller amounts but are crucial for overall health. Here are some essential micronutrients:

- **Vitamins**: Vitamins support various bodily functions, including immune function, energy production, and bone health.

  - Examples: Vitamin C (citrus fruits, strawberries), Vitamin D (sun exposure, fortified milk), Vitamin A (carrots, spinach), and B vitamins (whole grains, leafy greens).

- **Minerals**: Minerals are essential for building strong bones and teeth, regulating metabolism, and staying hydrated.

  - Examples: Calcium (dairy products, leafy greens), Iron (red meat, beans), Potassium (bananas, sweet potatoes), and Magnesium (nuts, seeds).

Hydration

Staying hydrated is vital for maintaining bodily functions, such as temperature regulation, joint lubrication, and nutrient transport. Aim to drink plenty of water throughout the day. The general recommendation is to drink at least eight glasses (64 ounces) of water daily. Still, your needs may vary based on activity level and climate.

Balanced Diet

A balanced diet includes a variety of foods from all food groups in the right proportions. Here's how to build a balanced plate:

- Half of Your Plate: Fill half your plate with fruits and vegetables. Aim for a colorful variety to ensure you get a range of nutrients.

- **One-Quarter of Your Plate**: Fill one-quarter of your plate with whole grains, such as brown rice, quinoa, or whole wheat bread.

- **One-Quarter of Your Plate**: Fill one-quarter of your plate with lean protein sources, such as chicken, fish, beans, or tofu.

- **Healthy Fats**: Include a small amount of healthy fats, such as a drizzle of olive oil, a handful of nuts, or slices of avocado.

Healthy Eating Tips

Here are some tips to help you develop healthy eating habits:

Plan Your Meals

Planning your meals helps you make healthier choices and get a balanced diet. Here's how to plan your meals:

- **Weekly Plan**: Create a weekly meal plan that includes a variety of foods from all food groups. Include breakfast, lunch, dinner, and snacks.

- Grocery List: Make a grocery list based on your meal plan. Stick to the list to avoid impulse purchases and ensure you have all the necessary ingredients.

- **Prep Ahead**: Prepare ingredients or meals ahead of time to save time during busy days. For example, chop vegetables, cook grains, or make a batch of soup.

Eat Mindfully

Mindful eating involves:

- Paying attention to what you eat.

- Savoring each bite.

- Listening to your body's hunger and fullness cues.Here's

How to practice mindful eating:

- **Slow Down**: Eat slowly and chew your food thoroughly. Take the time to enjoy the flavors and textures of your meal.

- **Avoid Distractions**: Avoid eating while watching TV, using your phone, or working. Focus on your meal and the experience of eating.

- **Listen to Your Body**: Pay attention to your body's signals of hunger and fullness. Eat when you're hungry and stop when you're satisfied.

Choose Healthy Snacks

Healthy snacks can provide energy and nutrients between meals. Here are some healthy snack ideas:

- **Fruits and Vegetables**: Fresh fruit, carrot sticks, cucumber slices, cherry tomatoes.

- **Protein-Rich Snacks**: Greek yogurt, hard-boiled eggs, hummus with veggie sticks, nuts, and seeds.

- **Whole Grains**: Whole grain crackers, air-popped popcorn, whole grain toast with avocado.

Limit Sugary and Processed Foods

Sugary and processed foods can contribute to weight gain and health issues. Here's how to limit these foods:

- **Read Labels**: Check food labels for added sugars and unhealthy fats. Choose products with minimal added sugars and ingredients.

- **Choose Whole Foods**: Opt for whole, unprocessed foods as much as possible. Fresh fruits, vegetables, whole grains, and lean proteins are healthier choices.

- **Healthy Alternatives**: Find more nutritious alternatives to your favorite sugary or processed foods. For example, replace sugary cereals with oatmeal topped with fruit or choose whole grain bread over white bread.

Understanding Exercise

Regular physical activity is crucial for maintaining a healthy body and mind. Exercise helps improve cardiovascular health, strength, flexibility, and mood. Here are the main types of exercise and their benefits:

Cardiovascular Exercise

Cardiovascular exercise, or cardio, increases your heart rate and improves your heart and lung health. Examples of cardio exercises include:

- **Running**: Great for building endurance and burning calories. You can run outdoors or on a treadmill.

- **Cycling**: Low-impact exercise that strengthens your legs and improves cardiovascular health. You can cycle outdoors or use a stationary bike.

- **Swimming**: A full-body workout that is easy on the joints and improves cardiovascular fitness.

- **Dancing**: This is a fun way to get your heart pumping while improving coordination and flexibility.

Strength Training

Strength training builds muscle strength and endurance. It also helps maintain bone density and improves metabolism. Examples of strength training exercises include:

- **Weightlifting**: Using dumbbells, barbells, or weight machines to perform squats, deadlifts, and bench presses.

- **Bodyweight Exercises**: These involve using your body weight for resistance, such as push-ups, pull-ups, lunges, and planks.

- **Resistance Bands**: Resistance bands can challenge exercises like bicep curls, shoulder presses, and leg lifts.

Flexibility and Balance Exercises

Flexibility and balance exercises help improve range of motion, reduce the risk of injury, and improve overall physical performance. Examples include:

- **Stretching**: Static stretches (holding a stretch for 15-30 seconds) and dynamic stretches (moving through a range of motion) improve flexibility.

- Yoga: Combines stretching, strength, and balance exercises to improve flexibility, reduce stress, and improve overall well-being.

- **Tai Chi**: Gentle, flowing movements that improve balance, coordination, and relaxation.

High-Intensity Interval Training (HIIT)

HIIT involves short bursts of intense exercise followed by periods of rest or low-intensity exercise. It's an efficient way to improve cardiovascular fitness and burn calories. Examples of HIIT workouts include:

- **Tabata**: A form of HIIT that involves 20 seconds of intense exercise followed by 10 seconds of rest, repeated for eight rounds.

- **Circuit Training**: Performing a series of exercises in a circuit with minimal rest between each exercise.

Creating an Exercise Routine

A balanced exercise routine helps you stay consistent and achieve your fitness goals. Here's how to create an effective exercise routine:

Set Fitness Goals

Set specific, achievable fitness goals to guide your exercise routine. Examples of fitness goals include:

- **Running a 5K**: Training to run a 5-kilometer race.

- **Building Muscle**: Increasing muscle strength and size through strength training.

- **Improving Flexibility**: Enhancing flexibility through regular stretching and yoga.

- **Weight Management**: Achieving or maintaining a healthy weight through cardio and strength training.

Plan Your Workouts

Plan your workouts to include a mix of cardio, strength training, and flexibility exercises. Here's a sample weekly workout plan:

- **Monday**: Cardio (running or cycling) + Full-body strength training.

- **Tuesday**: Yoga or stretching + Core workout.

- **Wednesday**: Cardio (swimming or dancing) + Upper body strength training.

- **Thursday**: Rest or light activity (walking or stretching).

- **Friday**: Cardio (HIIT or circuit training) + Lower body strength training.

- **Saturday**: Outdoor activity (hiking or playing a sport) + Flexibility exercises.

- **Sunday**: Rest or active recovery (gentle yoga or walking).

Warm Up and Cool Down

Always start your workouts with a warm-up and end with a cool-down. Warming up prepares your body for exercise and reduces the risk of injury. Cooling down helps your body recover and relieves muscle soreness. Here's how to warm up and cool down:

- **Warm-Up**: 5-10 minutes of light cardio (e.g., jogging, jumping jacks) followed by dynamic stretches (e.g., leg swings, arm circles).

- **Cool-Down**: 5-10 minutes of light cardio (e.g., walking) followed by static stretches (e.g., hamstring stretch, shoulder stretch).

Stay Consistent

Consistency is key to achieving your fitness goals. Here are some tips to stay consistent:

- **Schedule Workouts**: Schedule your workouts at the same time each day to build a routine.

- **Set Reminders**: Set reminders on your phone or calendar to stay on track.

- **Find a Workout Buddy**: Exercise with a friend or family member for motivation and accountability.

- **Track Progress**: Keep a workout journal or use a fitness app to track your progress and celebrate your achievements.

Mindfulness and Relaxation

Mental well-being is a crucial aspect of overall health, in addition to physical health. Mindfulness and relaxation techniques can help you manage stress, improve focus, and improve your overall quality of life. Let's explore some mindfulness and relaxation practices.

What is Mindfulness?

Mindfulness is being present and fully engaged in the current moment. It involves paying attention to your thoughts, feelings, and sensations without judgment. Mindfulness can help reduce stress, improve concentration, and promote emotional well-being.

Mindfulness Practices

Here are some mindfulness practices to incorporate into your daily routine:

Mindful Breathing

Mindful breathing involves focusing on and observing your breath without trying to change it. Here's how to practice conscious breathing:

- **Find a Quiet Space**: Sit or lie down in a comfortable position in a quiet space.

- **Focus on Your Breath**: Close your eyes and take slow, deep breaths. Focus on the sensation of the air entering and leaving your body.

- **Observe Your Thoughts**: If your mind starts to wander, gently bring your focus back to your breath. Observe your thoughts without judgment and let them pass.

Body Scan Meditation

Body scan meditation involves paying attention to different body parts and releasing tension. Here's how to practice a body scan meditation:

- **Find a Comfortable Position**: Lie down or sit in a comfortable position.

- **Focus on Your Breath**: Take a few deep breaths to relax.

- **Scan Your Body**: Slowly bring your attention to different body parts, starting from your toes and moving up to your head. Notice any sensations, tension, or discomfort.

- **Release Tension**: As you focus on each body part, consciously release tension and relax.

Mindful Walking

Mindful walking involves paying attention to the sensations of walking and your surroundings. Here's how to practice mindful walking:

- **Find a Quiet Place**: Choose a quiet place to walk, such as a park or a quiet street.

- **Walk Slowly**: Walk slowly and deliberately, paying attention to each step.

- **Observe Sensations**: Notice the sensation of your feet touching the ground, the movement of your legs, and the rhythm of your breath.

- **Be Present**: Observe your surroundings, such as the sights, sounds, and smells.

Mindful Eating

Mindful eating involves:

- Paying attention to the experience of eating.

- Savoring each bite.

- Listening to your body's hunger and fullness cues.Here's

How to practice mindful eating:

- **Eat Slowly**: Take your time to chew your food thoroughly and savor the flavors and textures.

- **Avoid Distractions**: Avoid eating while watching TV, using your phone, or working. Focus on your meal and the experience of eating.

- **Listen to Your Body**: Pay attention to your body's signals of hunger and fullness. Eat when you're hungry and stop when you're satisfied.

Relaxation Techniques

Relaxation techniques help reduce stress and promote a sense of calm and well-being. Here are some relaxation techniques to try:

Progressive Muscle Relaxation

Progressive muscle relaxation involves tensing and relaxing different muscle groups in your body. Here's how to practice progressive muscle relaxation:

- **Find a Comfortable Position**: Lie down or sit in a

comfortable position.

- **Focus on Your Breath**: Take a few deep breaths to relax.

- **Tense and Relax**: Starting with your toes, tense the muscles as tightly as possible for a few seconds, then relax them completely. Move up your body, tensing and relaxing each muscle group.

Visualization

Visualization involves imagining a peaceful and calming scene to help reduce stress and promote relaxation. Here's how to practice visualization:

- **Find a Quiet Space**: Sit or lie in a quiet, comfortable space.

- **Close Your Eyes**: Close your eyes and take a few deep breaths to relax.

- Think of a Calming Scene: Visualize a peaceful scene, such as a beach, forest, or mountain. Focus on the details, such as the sights, sounds, and smells.

- **Stay Present**: Stay in the scene for a few minutes, allowing yourself to relax and enjoy the experience fully.

Guided Meditation

Guided meditation involves listening to a recorded meditation that guides you through relaxation and mindfulness exercises. Here's how to practice guided meditation:

- **Find a Quiet Space**: Sit or lie in a quiet, comfortable space.

- **Choose a Meditation**: Choose a guided meditation that suits your needs. You can find guided meditations on apps, websites, or platforms like YouTube.

- **Listen and Relax**: Listen to the guided meditation and follow the instructions. Allow yourself to relax and fully engage in the experience.

Deep Breathing

Deep breathing involves taking slow, deep breaths to calm the mind and body. Here's how to practice deep breathing:

- **Find a Comfortable Position**: Sit or lie down in a comfortable position.

- **Inhale Deeply**: Take a slow, deep breath through your nose, filling your lungs.

- **Hold Your Breath**: Hold your breath for a few seconds.

- **Exhale Slowly**: Exhale slowly through your mouth, emptying your lungs.

- **Repeat**: Repeat the deep breathing for a few minutes,

focusing on the rhythm of your breath.

Incorporating Mindfulness and Relaxation into Daily Life

Incorporating mindfulness and relaxation practices into your daily life can help you manage stress and improve your overall well-being. Here's how to make mindfulness and relaxation a regular part of your routine:

Set Aside Time

Set aside time each day for mindfulness and relaxation practices. Even just a few minutes can make a difference. Schedule this time into your daily routine to make it a habit.

Create a Relaxing Environment

Create a relaxing environment for your mindfulness and relaxation practices. Choose a quiet space, dim the lights, and add calming elements such as soft music, candles, or essential oils.

Be Consistent

Consistency is key to reaping the benefits of mindfulness and relaxation. Practice regularly, even on busy days, to build a strong foundation for your well-being.

Stay Present

Stay present and fully engage in your mindfulness and relaxation practices. Avoid distractions and focus on the experience, allowing yourself to relax and unwind.

Reflect and Adjust

Reflect on your mindfulness and relaxation practices and how they impact your well-being. Adjust your practices as needed to suit your needs and preferences.

Healthy habits, including good nutrition, regular exercise, mindfulness, and relaxation, are essential for maintaining physical and mental well-being. Incorporating these practices into your daily routine allows you to feel your best, stay energized, and manage stress effectively.

Remember, building healthy habits takes time and effort. Stay patient, stay consistent, and keep learning. With the knowledge and strategies you've learned in this chapter, you have the strength to create a healthy, balanced, and fulfilling life, Supergirl!

CHAPTER FOURTEEN

Exploring Creativity

Finding Your Passion

Hello, Supergirl! Creativity is a wonderful and strengthful aspect of being human. It allows us to express ourselves, solve problems, and see the world differently. Exploring creativity can help you discover your passions and develop skills that bring joy and fulfillment. This section will explore finding your passion and engaging in creative expression activities. Let's get started!

Why Creativity Matters

Creativity is essential for several reasons:

Self-Expression: Creativity allows you to express your thoughts, feelings, and ideas uniquely.

Problem-Solving: Creative thinking helps you find innovative solutions to problems and challenges.

Personal Growth: Engaging in creative activities promotes individual growth and self-discovery.

Stress Relief: Creative activities can be relaxing and therapeutic, helping manage stress and improve mental well-being.

Joy and Fulfillment: Creativity brings joy and fulfillment by allowing you to engage in activities that you're passionate about.

Finding Your Passion

Finding your passion involves exploring different interests and discovering what brings you joy and fulfillment. Here are some steps to help you find your love:

Reflect on Your Interests

Start by reflecting on your interests and activities that excite and engage you. Here are some questions to consider:

- What activities do you enjoy doing in your free time?

- What topics do you love learning about?

- What hobbies or interests have you always wanted to try?

- What activities make you lose track of time because you're so immersed in them?

Write down your answers to these questions to gain insight into your interests and potential passions.

Explore New Activities

Exploring new activities can help you discover interests and passions you may not have considered. Here are some ways to explore new activities:

- **Try New Hobbies**: Experiment with different hobbies, such as painting, writing, playing a musical instrument, cooking, gardening, or crafting. Don't hesitate to step out of your comfort zone and try something new.

- **Attend Workshops and Classes**: Sign up for workshops, classes, or online courses to learn new skills and explore different activities. Many community centers, libraries, and online platforms offer courses on various topics.

- **Volunteer**: Volunteering is a great way to explore new interests while making a positive impact. Look for volunteer opportunities in areas that interest you, such as animal shelters, community gardens, or arts organizations.

Identify Your Strengths

Your strengths and talents can provide clues to your passions. Here's how to identify your strengths:

- **Reflect on Past Successes**: Think about activities or

projects you've excelled in and enjoyed. What skills did you use, and what aspects did you find most rewarding?

- Seek Feedback: Ask friends, family, teachers, or mentors about your strengths and talents. This can offer valuable insights and perspectives.

- **Take Assessments**: Consider taking assessments or quizzes that help identify your strengths and interests. Many online tools can provide insights into your personality, strengths, and potential career paths.

Follow Your Curiosity

Curiosity is a strong driver of passion. Follow your curiosity by exploring topics and activities that pique your interest. Here's how to nurture your curiosity:

- **Read Widely**: Read books, articles, and blogs on interesting topics. Explore different genres and subjects to expand your knowledge and spark new ideas.

- **Watch Documentaries and Talks**: Watch documentaries, TED Talks, and educational videos on topics that intrigue you. These can provide inspiration and new perspectives.

- **Ask Questions**: Be bold, ask questions, and seek answers. Curiosity-driven learning can lead to new interests and passions.

Reflect and Evaluate

Regularly reflect on your experiences and evaluate how they align with your interests and passions. Here's how to reflect and assess:

- **Keep a Journal**: Keep a journal to document your experiences, thoughts, and feelings as you explore different activities. Reflect on what you enjoyed, what you learned, and how each activity made you feel.

- **Assess Your Fulfillment**: Evaluate how fulfilled and satisfied you feel after engaging in different activities. Activities that align with your passions will likely bring joy and fulfillment.

- **Adjust and Adapt**: Be open to adjusting and adapting your interests and passions as you grow and learn. Your passions may evolve, and that's perfectly normal.

Creative Expression Activities

Once you've identified your interests and passions, engaging in creative expression activities can help you explore and develop your creativity. Here are some creative expression activities to try:

Visual Arts

Visual arts encompass a wide range of activities that involve creating visual works of art. Here are some visual arts activities to explore:

- **Drawing and Painting**: Experiment with different drawing and painting techniques, such as sketching, watercolors, acrylics, and oil painting. Create landscapes, portraits, abstract art, or still lifes.

- **Sculpting**: Try sculpting with clay, playdough, or other materials. Create sculptures of animals, people, or abstract forms.

- **Photography**: Explore photography by capturing images of nature, people, architecture, or everyday objects. Experiment with different angles, lighting, and composition.

- **Digital Art**: Create digital art using software and apps. Experiment with digital painting, graphic design, and photo manipulation.

Performing Arts

Performing arts involves expressing creativity through performance. Here are some performing arts activities to try:

- **Music**: Learn to play a musical instrument, such as the piano, guitar, violin, or drums. Then, experiment with composing your music or playing your favorite songs.

- **Singing**: Take singing lessons or join a choir to develop your vocal skills. Sing along to your favorite songs or perform for friends and family.

- **Dance**: Explore different dance styles, such as ballet, hip-hop, jazz, contemporary, or ballroom. Take dance classes or follow online tutorials.

- **Theater**: Participate in theater productions or drama classes. Practice acting, improvisation, and stage performance.

Literary Arts

Literary arts involve expressing creativity through writing and storytelling. Here are some literary arts activities to explore:

- **Creative Writing**: Write short stories, poems, essays, or novels. Experiment with different genres like fantasy, mystery, romance, or science fiction.

- **Journaling**: Keep a journal to document your thoughts, feelings, and experiences. Use journaling as a tool for self-reflection and personal growth.

- **Scriptwriting**: Write scripts for plays, movies, or TV shows. Develop characters, plotlines, and dialogue.

- **Blogging**: Start a blog to share your writing, ideas, and experiences with others. Choose a topic you're passionate about and create engaging content.

Crafts and DIY Projects

Crafts and DIY projects involve creating handmade items and exploring different crafting techniques. Here are some crafts and DIY activities to try:

- **Knitting and Crocheting**: Learn to knit or crochet to create scarves, hats, blankets, and other handmade items. Experiment with different patterns and yarns.

- **Sewing**: Try sewing to create clothing, accessories, or home decor items. Experiment with different fabrics and sewing techniques.

- **Jewelry Making**: Create your jewelry using beads, wire, and other materials: design necklaces, bracelets, earrings, and rings.

- **Paper Crafts**: Explore paper crafts such as origami, scrapbooking, and card making. Create intricate paper designs and personalized gifts.

Culinary Arts

Culinary arts involve expressing creativity through cooking and baking. Here are some culinary arts activities to explore:

- **Cooking**: Experiment with different cuisines and recipes. Try cooking new dishes, experimenting with flavors, and creating your recipes.

- **Baking**: Explore baking by making cakes, cookies, bread, and pastries. Decorate your baked goods with icing, fondant, and other decorations.

- **Food Presentation**: Experiment with food presentation and plating techniques. Create visually appealing dishes and experiment with garnishes and decorations.

- **Food Photography**: Capture beautiful images of your culinary creations. Experiment with lighting, composition, and styling.

Nurturing Your Creativity

Nurturing your creativity involves creating an environment that encourages and supports creative expression. Here are some tips for nurturing your creativity:

Create a Creative Space

Designate a space in your home to focus on your creative activities. Here's how to create an innovative space:

- **Choose a Quiet Area**: Choose a quiet area with minimal distractions. If available, this could be a corner of your room, a desk, or a separate room.

- **Organize Your Supplies**: Keep your creative supplies organized and easily accessible. Use storage containers, shelves, and drawers to store your materials.

- **Personalize Your Space**: Decorate your creative space with inspiring items, such as artwork, photos, and motivational quotes.

Set Aside Time for Creativity

Make creativity a routine by setting aside time for creative activities. Here's how to set aside time for creativity:

- **Schedule Creative Time**: Schedule regular time slots for creative activities, such as an hour each day or a few hours each week. Treat this time as important and non-negotiable.

- **Eliminate Distractions**: During your creative time, eliminate distractions such as phones, social media, and TV. Focus solely on your creative activity.

- **Be Consistent**: Consistency is key to developing your creativity. Make creativity a habit by engaging in creative activities regularly.

Seek Inspiration

Inspiration can come from many sources. Here's how to seek inspiration for your creative activities:

- **Explore Nature**: Spend time in nature to find inspiration in the beauty and tranquility of the natural world. Observe the colors, shapes, and textures around you.

- **Visit Museums and Galleries**: Visit museums, galleries, and exhibitions to see works of art and gain inspiration from different artists and styles.

- **Read and Watch**: Read books, articles, and blogs on interesting topics. Watch documentaries, movies, and shows that inspire and motivate you.

- **Connect with Others**: Connect with other creative individuals to share ideas, collaborate, and gain inspiration. Join creative communities, attend workshops, and participate in online forums.

Embrace Mistakes

Creativity involves experimentation and taking risks, which can sometimes lead to mistakes. Here's how to embrace mistakes in your creative process:

- **View Mistakes as Learning Opportunities**: Instead of seeing mistakes as failures, view them as opportunities to learn and grow. Reflect on what you can learn from each mistake and how to improve.

- **Experiment and Take Risks**: Don't be afraid to experiment and take risks in your creative activities. Trying new techniques and pushing boundaries can lead to unexpected and exciting results.

- **Celebrate Imperfections**: Embrace the imperfections in your creative work. Sometimes, the most unique and interesting creations come from imperfections and mistakes.

Stay Positive and Encouraged

Maintaining a positive attitude and staying encouraged is essential for nurturing your creativity. Here's how to stay positive and encouraged:

- **Celebrate Small Wins**: Celebrate your achievements and progress, no matter how small. Recognize and appreciate your efforts and successes.

- **Stay Motivated**: Set goals and rewards to stay motivated and focused. Break larger projects into smaller tasks and reward yourself for completing them.

- **Seek Support**: Surround yourself with supportive friends, family, and mentors who encourage and inspire you. Share your creative journey with them and seek their feedback and support.

Exploring Different Creative Fields

Creativity spans a wide range of fields and disciplines. Exploring creative fields can help you discover new interests and expand your skills. Here are some creative fields to explore:

Visual Arts

The visual arts encompass various activities, from traditional fine arts to modern digital art. Here are some visual arts fields to explore:

- **Fine Arts**: Includes drawing, painting, sculpting, and printmaking. Experiment with different mediums and techniques to express your creativity.

- **Graphic Design**: Combines art and technology to create visual content for print and digital media. Learn to use design software and create logos, posters, and websites.

- **Photography**: Captures images using cameras and editing software. Explore different photography styles, such as portrait, landscape, and street photography.

- **Animation**: Creates moving images through techniques like hand-drawn animation, stop-motion, and computer-generated imagery (CGI).

Performing Arts

The performing arts involve expressing creativity through performance. Here are some performing arts fields to explore:

- **Music**: Involves playing instruments, singing, composing, and producing music. Experiment with different genres and styles.

- **Dance**: Combines movement and music to express emotions and tell stories. Explore different dance styles and techniques.

- **Theater**: Involves acting, directing, and producing plays and performances. Participate in theater productions and drama classes.

- **Film and Media**: Combines storytelling, visual arts, and technology to create movies, TV shows, and digital content.

Literary Arts

The literary arts involve expressing creativity through writing and storytelling. Here are some literary arts fields to explore:

- **Fiction Writing**: Creates imaginative stories with characters, plots, and settings. Experiment with different genres like fantasy, mystery, and science fiction.

- **Non-Fiction Writing**: Involves writing factual content, such as essays, articles, and memoirs. Explore topics you're passionate about and share your insights and experiences.

- **Poetry**: Uses language, rhythm, and imagery to create expressive and evocative works. Experiment with different forms and styles of poetry.

- **Scriptwriting**: Writes scripts for plays, movies, and TV shows. Develop characters, dialogue, and plotlines for performance.

Crafts and DIY Projects

Crafts and DIY projects involve creating handmade items and exploring different crafting techniques. Here are some crafts and DIY fields to explore:

- **Textile Arts** include knitting, crocheting, sewing, and quilting. You can create clothing, accessories, and home decor items using these techniques.

- **Jewelry Making**: Design and create jewelry using beads, wire, and metal. Experiment with different techniques and styles.

- **Woodworking**: Involves creating items from wood, such as furniture, decor, and sculptures. Learn to use woodworking tools and techniques.

- **Paper Crafts**: Includes activities like origami, scrapbooking, and card making. Create intricate paper designs and personalized gifts.

Culinary Arts

The culinary arts involve expressing creativity through cooking and baking. Here are some culinary arts fields to explore:

- **Cooking**: Involves preparing and experimenting with different cuisines and recipes. Create savory dishes and explore different cooking techniques.

- **Baking**: Focuses on making baked goods like cakes, cookies, bread, and pastries. Experiment with flavors, decorations, and presentation.

- **Food Styling**: Combines cooking and visual arts to create visually appealing dishes. Experiment with plating techniques and food photography.

- **Mixology**: Involves creating and experimenting with drinks and cocktails. Learn to mix flavors and create unique beverages.

Exploring creativity and finding your passion are essential for personal growth and fulfillment. By reflecting on your interests, trying new activities, and engaging in creative expression, you can discover what brings you joy and develop skills that enrich your life.

Remember, creativity is a journey, not a destination. Stay curious, stay open-minded, and embrace the process of exploration and discovery. With the knowledge and strategies you've learned in this chapter, you have the strength to unlock your creativity and pursue your passions, Supergirl!

CHAPTER FIFTEEN

Setting Goals and Planning for the Future

Short-Term and Long-Term Goals

Hello, Supergirl! Setting goals and planning for the future is an exciting and essential part of your personal growth and development. Goals give you direction, motivation, and a sense of purpose. By setting short-term and long-term goals, you can create a roadmap to achieve your dreams and build your desired life. This section will explore how to set effective goals, the difference between short-term and long-term goals, and how to create a vision board to visualize your aspirations. Let's explore in!

Why Setting Goals Matters

Setting goals is crucial for several reasons:

Direction: Goals provide a clear direction and focus for your efforts.

Motivation: Working towards goals keeps you motivated and driven.

Accountability: Goals hold you accountable and help you track your progress.

Personal Growth: Achieving goals fosters personal growth and self-improvement.

Fulfillment: Reaching your goals brings a sense of accomplishment and fulfillment.

Types of Goals

There are different types of goals, each serving a unique purpose in your journey. Here are the main types of goals:

Short-Term Goals

Short-term goals are goals you aim to achieve shortly, typically within a few days, weeks, or months. These are often stepping stones toward your long-term goals. Examples of short-term goals include:

- Completing a school project by the end of the week.

- Learning a new skill, such as playing a song on the guitar, within a month.

- Reading a book or finishing a book series within two weeks.

- Improving your grades in a particular subject by the end of the semester.

Long-Term Goals

Long-term goals are goals you aim to achieve over an extended period, typically several months, years, or even a lifetime. These often require sustained effort and commitment. Examples of long-term goals include:

- Graduating from high school with honors.

- Getting accepted into your dream college or university.

- Pursuing a specific career, such as becoming a doctor, engineer, or artist.

- Saving money for a significant purchase, such as a car or a trip abroad.

- Maintaining a healthy lifestyle and achieving fitness milestones.

How to Set Effective Goals

Setting effective goals involves more than just deciding what you want to achieve. It requires careful planning and consideration. Here's how to set goals effectively:

Use the SMART Criteria

The SMART criteria ensure your goals are clear, realistic, and achievable. Here's what SMART stands for:

- **Specific**: Clearly define what you want to achieve. Avoid vague or general goals. For example, instead of saying, "I want to get fit," say, "I want to run a 5K race in six months."

- **Measurable**: Make sure your Goal is measurable so you can track your progress. Include specific metrics or milestones. For example, "I want to improve my math grade from a B to an A by the end of the semester."

- **Achievable**: Set goals that are challenging but attainable. Consider your current abilities and resources. For example, "I want to learn to play three songs on the guitar within two months" is achievable with regular practice.

- **Relevant**: Ensure your goals are relevant to your interests, values, and long-term aspirations. For example, if you're passionate about writing, an appropriate goal might be, "I want to write and publish a short story by the end of the year."

- **Time-Bound**: Set a specific deadline for achieving your Goal. This adds a sense of urgency and helps you stay focused. For example, "I want to save $500 for a trip by next summer."

Break Down Your Goals

Breaking down your goals into smaller, manageable steps makes them less overwhelming and easier to achieve. Here's how to break down your goals:

- **Identify Major Milestones**: Determine the key milestones you must achieve to reach your Goal. For example, if your Goal is to run a 5K, major milestones include running 1K, 3K, and 5K.

- **Create Action Steps**: Outline the specific actions you must take to reach each milestone. For example, your Goal is to improve your math grade. In that case, action steps include studying for 30 minutes daily, attending extra help sessions, and completing practice problems.

- **Set Deadlines**: Assign deadlines to each action step to ensure steady progress. For example, "Complete the first draft of my short story by the end of the month."

Write Down Your Goals

Writing down your goals makes them more tangible and helps you stay committed. Here's how to document your goals:

- **Create a Goal Journal**: Write down your goals, action steps, and deadlines in a notebook or digital journal. Review and update your journal regularly to track your progress.

- **Use Goal-Setting Apps**: Consider using goal-setting apps that help you set, track, and achieve your goals. Popular apps include Todoist, Trello, and GoalsOnTrack.

- **Visual Reminders**: Place visual reminders of your goals in prominent places, such as your bedroom, study area, or phone. This keeps your goals top of mind.

Stay Motivated and Accountable

Staying motivated and accountable is crucial for achieving your goals. Here's how to keep on track:

- **Find a Goal Buddy**: Share your goals with a friend, family member, or mentor who can provide support and accountability. Regularly check in with each other to discuss progress and challenges.

- **Reward Yourself**: Set up a reward system to celebrate your achievements, no matter how small. Rewards, such as treating yourself to a favorite snack or activity, can be simple.

- **Reflect on Progress**: Regularly reflect on your progress and adjust your action plan. Celebrate your successes and learn from any setbacks.

Creating a Vision Board

A vision board is a strong tool for visualizing your goals and dreams. It constantly reminds you of what you want to achieve and helps keep you focused and motivated. Here's how to create a vision board:

What is a Vision Board?

A vision board collages of images, words, and quotes representing your goals and aspirations. It visually expresses what you want to achieve and serves as a daily reminder to stay focused and motivated.

Steps to Create a Vision Board

Gather Supplies

To create your vision board, you'll need the following supplies:

- **Poster Board or Corkboard**: Choose a sturdy surface for your vision board. A poster board or corkboard works well.

- **Magazines and Printed Images**: Gather magazines, printed images, and photos representing your goals and dreams.

- **Scissors and Glue**: Use scissors to cut out pictures and words and glue or pins to attach to your board.

- **Markers and Stickers**: Use markers, stickers, and other decorative items to personalize your vision board.

Define Your Goals and Dreams

Before you start creating your vision board, take some time to reflect on your goals and dreams. Here are some areas to consider:

- **Personal Growth**: Goals related to self-improvement, such as learning new skills, developing healthy habits, or building confidence.

- **Career and Education**: Goals related to your education, career aspirations, and professional development.

- **Health and Fitness**: Physical health, fitness, and overall well-being goals.

- **Relationships**: Goals related to building and maintaining positive relationships with family, friends, and peers.

- **Hobbies and Interests**: Goals related to pursuing hobbies, interests, and creative activities.

- **Travel and Adventure**: Goals related to travel, exploring new places, and seeking adventure.

Collect Images and Words

Collect images, words, and quotes that represent your goals and dreams. Here's how to find inspiration:

- **Magazines**: Flip through magazines and cut out images and words that resonate with you.

- **Online Sources**: Search for images and quotes, and print out those that inspire you.

- **Personal Photos**: Include photos representing your goals, such as a picture of a place you want to visit or an activity you want to try.

Arrange and Attach

Arrange the images, words, and quotes on your board in a meaningful and inspiring way. Here's how to arrange and attach your items:

- **Create Categories**: Group similar goals and dreams together. For example, create personal growth, health and fitness, and travel sections.

- **Layer and Overlap**: Layer and overlap images and words to create a visually appealing collage. Don't worry about perfecting it; focus on what feels right.

- **Attach with** glue or pins: Securely attach your items to the board with glue or pins. Add decorative elements like stickers, washi tape, and drawings to personalize your vision board.

Display Your Vision Board

Place your vision board in a prominent place where you'll see it regularly. Here are some ideas for displaying your vision board:

- **Bedroom or Study Area**: Hang your vision board in your bedroom or study area to see it daily.

- **Digital Vision Board**: Create a digital version of your vision board and set it as your computer or phone wallpaper.

- **Bulletin Board**: Post your vision board on a bulletin board in a common area, such as your kitchen or living room, to share it with family or roommates.

Using Your Vision Board

Your vision board is a dynamic tool that can evolve as you grow and change. Here's how to use and maintain your vision board:

Regularly Review

Review your vision board regularly to stay focused and motivated. Take a few minutes daily to look at your vision board and visualize achieving your goals.

Update and Refresh

As you achieve and set new goals, update and refresh your vision board. Add new images and words that represent your evolving aspirations.

Reflect and Celebrate

Reflect on your progress and celebrate your achievements. Use your vision board as a reminder of how far you've come and the goals you've accomplished.

Stay Positive

Stay positive and believe in your ability to achieve your goals. Use your vision board to reinforce a positive mindset and remind yourself of your potential.

Goal-Setting and Planning Tools

In addition to vision boards, various tools and techniques can help you set and achieve your goals. Here are some useful goal-setting and planning tools:

Goal Journals and Planners

Goal journals and planners help you document your goals, action steps, and progress. Here are some features to look for:

- **Daily, Weekly, and Monthly Layouts**: Look for journals and planners with daily, weekly, and monthly layouts to plan and track your goals.

- **Reflection Prompts**: Choose journals with reflection prompts to help you evaluate your progress and stay motivated.

- **Action Plans**: Look for planners with sections for creating action plans and setting deadlines.

Digital Apps and Tools

Digital apps and tools can help you set, track, and achieve your goals. Here are some popular options:

- **Todoist**: A task management app that helps you set goals, create to-do lists, and track progress.

- **Trello**: A project management tool that uses boards, lists, and cards to organize tasks and track milestones.

- **GoalsOnTrack**: A goal-setting and tracking app that helps you set SMART goals, create action plans, and monitor your progress.

- **Habitica**: A habit-tracking app that gamifies your goals and habits, making goal-setting fun and engaging.

Mind Mapping

Mind mapping is a visual technique that helps you brainstorm and organize your goals and ideas. Here's how to create a mind map:

- **Central Idea**: Write your main Goal or theme in the center of the page.

- **Branches**: Draw branches from the central idea for each major Goal or category.

- **Sub-Branches**: Add sub-branches for specific action steps, tasks, and milestones.

- **Visual Elements**: Use colors, images, and symbols to make your mind map visually appealing and easy to understand.

Accountability Partners

An accountability partner supports and motivates you to achieve your goals. Here's how to work with an accountability partner:

- **Choose a Partner**: Choose someone you trust with similar goals or interests.

- **Set Regular Check-Ins**: Schedule regular check-ins to discuss your progress, challenges, and achievements.

- **Provide Support**: Offer support and encouragement to each other. Share resources, tips, and feedback to help each other stay on track.

Examples of Short-Term and Long-Term Goals

To give you a better knowledge of how to set effective goals, here are some examples of short-term and long-term goals:

Short-Term Goals

Academic Goal: "I want to improve my math grade from a B to an A by the end of the semester."

1. **Action Steps**: Study for 30 minutes daily, attend extra help sessions, complete practice problems, and review notes regularly.

2. **Deadline**: End of the semester.

3. **Health Goal**: "I want to run a 5K race in three months."

   ○ **Action Steps**: Follow a 5K training plan, run thrice weekly, gradually increase distance, and cross-train with strength exercises.

   ○ **Deadline**: Three months from now.

4. **Creative Goal**: "I want to paint a landscape within a month."

   ○ **Action Steps**: Gather painting supplies, choose a reference photo, sketch the composition, and paint for one hour daily.

   ○ **Deadline**: End of the month.

Long-Term Goals

1. **Educational Goal**: "I want to graduate from high school with honors."

   ○ **Action Steps**: Maintain a high GPA, complete all assignments on time, participate in extracurricular activities, and seek academic support when needed.

- ○ **Deadline**: High school graduation.

2. **Career Goal**: "I want to become a registered nurse."

- ○ **Action Steps**: Research nursing programs, complete prerequisite courses, apply to nursing schools, gain clinical experience, and pass the NCLEX-RN exam.

- ○ **Deadline**: Five years from now.

3. **Financial Goal**: "I want to save $10,000 for a down payment on a house."

- ○ **Action Steps**: Create a savings plan, set aside a portion of each paycheck, reduce unnecessary expenses, and explore additional income opportunities.

- ○ **Deadline**: Five years from now.

Setting goals and planning for the future are essential for achieving your dreams and living a fulfilling life. By setting short-term and long-term goals, using effective goal-setting strategies, and creating a vision board, you can stay focused, motivated, and on track to achieve your aspirations.

Remember, setting goals is just the beginning. Stay committed, stay positive, and believe in your ability to achieve your dreams. With the knowledge and strategies you've learned in this chapter, you have the strength to set meaningful goals and create a bright future, Supergirl!

CHAPTER SIXTEEN

Closing Thoughts

Hello, Supergirl! As we end this journey together, it's essential to reflect on all the valuable insights, tips, and strategies we've explored. Whether it's learning your emotions, sharpening your communication skills, building strong relationships, or setting goals for the future, each chapter has been designed to strengthen you and help you become the best version of yourself.

Embracing the Journey

Life is a journey filled with growth, learning, and self-discovery opportunities. Embrace every experience with an open mind and heart. Remember that every challenge you face is an opportunity to develop new skills, gain wisdom, and build resilience. Here are some key takeaways to keep in mind as you navigate through life:

1. **Self-Discovery**: Continually explore your interests and

passions. Self-discovery is an ongoing process, and remaining curious and open to new experiences is essential.

2. **Emotional Intelligence**: Understanding and managing emotions is crucial for personal and interpersonal success. Practice mindfulness, empathy, and effective communication to build strong, meaningful relationships.

3. **Confidence and Resilience**: Believe in yourself and your abilities. Confidence comes from self-acceptance and the courage to face your fears. Resilience is about bouncing back from setbacks and learning from your experiences.

4. **Healthy Habits**: Maintain a balanced lifestyle by prioritizing your physical and mental well-being. Healthy habits such as regular exercise, proper nutrition, and mindfulness are the foundation for a fulfilling life.

5. **Creativity and Passion**: Engage in creative activities that bring you joy and allow you to express yourself. Pursuing your passions will bring a sense of purpose and fulfillment to your life.

6. **Goal-Setting and Planning**: Set clear, achievable goals and create a roadmap for your future. Stay focused, motivated, and committed to your aspirations.

Gratitude and Reflection

Take a moment to express gratitude for the journey you've undertaken. Reflect on the progress you've made, the challenges you've overcome, and the lessons you've learned. Gratitude is a strengthful practice that can improve your well-being and foster a positive mindset. Here are some ways to incorporate gratitude and reflection into your daily life:

1. **Gratitude Journal**: Keep a gratitude journal where you write down three things you are grateful for daily. This simple practice can shift your focus to the positive aspects of your life.

2. **Reflection Time**: Set aside weekly time to reflect on your experiences, goals, and personal growth. Consider what you've learned and how to apply these insights moving forward.

3. **Celebrate Achievements**: Celebrate your achievements, no matter how small. Recognize your efforts and successes as stepping stones towards your larger goals.

Thank You and Best Wishes

Dear Supergirl,

Thank you for starting on this journey of self-discovery and growth. Your dedication to learning, improving, and becoming the best version of yourself is truly inspiring. It's been an honor to guide you through these chapters and share valuable insights to help you navigate life's challenges and opportunities.

Remember that you are capable of achieving great things. Believe in yourself, stay true to your values, and never stop pursuing your dreams. Life will present you with many paths, and each choice you make will shape your unique journey. Embrace every moment with courage, resilience, and a positive mindset.

As you continue your path, know that you have the strength to make a difference in the world. Your kindness, creativity, and determination can inspire others and create a ripple effect of positive change. Stay curious, stay passionate, and always strive for excellence.

Best wishes for a bright and fulfilling future. You are a true Supergirl; the world is lucky to have you.

CHAPTER SEVENTEEN

Recommended Resources and References

To continue your journey of self-improvement and personal growth, here are some recommended resources and references that you may find helpful:

Books

1. "The 7 Habits of Highly Effective Teens" by Sean Covey

- A practical and engaging guide that helps teenagers develop essential habits for success in life.

2. "Mindset: The New Psychology of Success" by Carol S. Dweck

- Explores the concept of a growth mindset and how it can

lead to greater achievement and fulfillment.

3. **"The Power of Now: A Guide to Spiritual Enlightenment" by Eckhart Tolle**

   ○ It is a transformative book that teaches the importance of living in the present moment and finding inner peace.

4. **"The Happiness Project" by Gretchen Rubin**

   ○ Chronicles the author's year-long journey to increase her happiness and provides practical advice for readers.

5. **"Daring Greatly: How the Courage to Be Vulnerable Transforms the Way We Live, Love, Parent, and Lead" by Brené Brown**

   ○ Explores the strength of vulnerability and how embracing it can lead to a more authentic and fulfilling life.

Online Resources

1. **Khan Academy** (www.khanacademy.org)

   ○ A comprehensive online platform offering free courses on various subjects, including math, science, and humanities.

2. **TED-Ed** (www.ed.ted.com)

- It provides educational videos and lessons on various topics created by educators and animators.

3. **Mindful Schools** (www.mindfulschools.org)

- Offers resources and courses on mindfulness for students, educators, and parents.

4. **Coursera** (www.coursera.org)

- An online learning platform that offers courses from top universities and institutions on various subjects.

5. **Headspace** (www.headspace.com)

- A mindfulness and meditation app that provides guided meditation sessions to help manage stress and improve well-being.

Apps

1. **Todoist**

- A task management app that helps you set goals, create to-do lists, and track your progress.

2. **Trello**

- A project management tool that uses boards, lists, and cards to organize tasks and track milestones.

3. GoalsOnTrack

- A goal-setting and tracking app that helps you set SMART goals, create action plans, and monitor your progress.

4. Habitica

- A habit-tracking app that gamifies your goals and habits, making goal-setting fun and engaging.

5. Calm

- A mindfulness and meditation app that offers guided meditation, sleep stories, and relaxation techniques.

Websites

1. Positive Psychology (www.positivepsychology.com)

- Provides articles, courses, and resources on positive psychology and well-being.

2. Verywell Mind (www.verywellmind.com)

- Offers articles and resources on mental health, self-improvement, and emotional well-being.

3. Psychology Today (www.psychologytoday.com)

- Features articles, blogs, and resources on psychology, mental health, and self-help.

4. **The Muse** (www.themuse.com)

- Offers career advice, job search resources, and professional development tips.

5. **Art of Charm** (www.theartofcharm.com)

- Provides resources and podcasts on social skills, confidence, and personal development.

Final Words

As you move forward, remember that the journey of self-discovery and personal growth is ongoing. Continue to seek knowledge, embrace new experiences, and stay committed to your goals. You can create a life filled with purpose, joy, and fulfillment.

Stay inspired, stay motivated, and never stop believing in yourself. The future is bright, and you have the potential to achieve greatness. Keep shining, Supergirl!

With endless encouragement and best wishes,

Made in United States
Troutdale, OR
11/27/2024